*The Book of Gold*
*Le Livre d'Or*

Published by Avalonia

BM Avalonia
London
WC1N 3XX
England, UK

www.avaloniabooks.co.uk

'The Book of Gold'
Being a partial transcription of Lansdowne MS1202, translated by Paul Harry Barron from the original French, Introduced by David Rankine, with commentary by David Rankine & Paul Harry Barron.

ISBN-10: 1-905297-28-9
ISBN-13: 978-1-905297-28-3

First PB Edition, May 2010
Design by Satori

Cover Art "David & The Devil" (King David in penitence before God, who is seen blessing in the sky. Behind David stands the Devil, who has big horns, a face on his groin, and the legs of a chicken. Psalm 38), taken from Breviary of John the Fearless, published in Paris in French and Latin between 1413-1419, illustration by Master of Guillebert de Metz. With the Kind Permission of the British Library in London.

British Library Cataloguing in Publication Data. A catalogue record for this book is available from the British Library.

*"The which Psalms, are nothing else,*
*but a means unto the seat and  Majesty of God:*
*whereby you gather with yourselves due power,*
*to apply your natures to the holy Angels"*

The archangel Uriel to Dr John Dee, March 10th 1582.

# THE BOOK OF GOLD

A 17TH CENTURY MAGICAL GRIMOIRE OF AMULETS, CHARMS, PRAYERS, SIGILS AND SPELLS USING THE BIBLICAL PSALMS OF KING DAVID

DAVID RANKINE
& PAUL HARRY BARRON

PUBLISHED BY AVALONIA

WWW.AVALONIABOOKS.CO.UK

# ACKNOWLEDGEMENTS

We would like to thank Stephen Blake for his invaluable assistance with the manuscript.

Thank you to the staff at the British Library for their assistance with the text and cover image.

Sorita d'Este for her encouragement, editorial advice and for being a Muse.

Joseph Peterson, whose translation of *Sepher Shimmush Tehillim* in his seminal edition of *The Sixth and Seventh Books of Moses* was invaluable in our research.

John Canard for bringing some of the traditional European folk magic uses to our attention.

Stephen Skinner for his ongoing support and fascinating discussions of all things grimoire-related.

*"The words of the Lord are pure words: as silver tried by the fire, purged from the earth refined seven times."*
*Psalm 11.7*

# TABLE OF CONTENTS

# Introduction

The Book of Psalms is the longest book in the Bible, and arguably the most magical. The one hundred and fifty Psalms have been used as the basis of amulets and for magical assistance for many centuries, with evidence of their use for apotropaic, healing and coercive magic dating back at least as far as the third century CE. Fragments from the *Cairo Genizah* and the *Dead Sea Scrolls* show that the Psalms were considered extremely powerful manifestations of divine power, with the incipits (opening lines) often being used as symbols of the power contained within the whole Psalm.

Whilst we do not intend to attempt to trace the Psalms back to their roots, it is clear from their style and content that they were heavily influenced by Babylonian and Egyptian hymns and prayers, and to an extent could thus be viewed as continuing the magical traditions of these cultures.[1] This is a logical conclusion when we recall the two periods of captivity for the Hebrews were with these two civilizations.

With the cross-fertilization of ideas between the Jewish, Hellenic and Gnostic practices of the first-fourth century CE, the Psalms soon found their way into other magical systems. There are references in Greek texts such as the *Greek Magical Papyri* which indicate the influence of the Psalms

---

[1] See The Psalms as Liturgies, Peters, 2009.

there in the fourth and fifth century CE. Thus we see fragmentary phrases which seem to be drawn from the Psalms in e.g. *A tested charm of Pibechis for those possessed by daimons* (PGM IV.3007-86), including Ps 103:32 (3076), Ps 113.3 (3055), and Ps 134:7 (3066).

Instructions are also given which indicate the commanding power of the Psalms, such as: *"Continue without deception, lord, the vision of every act, in accordance with the command of the holy spirit, the angel of Phoibos, you yourself being pliable because of these songs and psalms"* (PGM III.287-88).[2]

Another significant feature of the Psalms is that their magic transcends language, with charms, prayers and spells being found in numerous languages including Aramaic, English, French Greek, Hebrew, Latin, Runes and Russian.

The Psalms featured prominently in early Christian magic. Of the ninety-three Christian amulets from the period fourth-eighth century CE written on parchment or papyrus, *"at least thirty-one of the amulets quote from the Psalms, most of which are from Psalm 90 or Psalm 1."*[3]

The first major text focusing entirely on the magical use of the Psalms is the Hebrew *Sepher Shimmush Tehillim* (*Magical Use of the Psalms*) which dates back to the eighth century CE. Although there are no known copies of this text until centuries later, we have contemporary references to it which indicate an early form of *Sepher Shimmush Tehillim* did exist and was used at this time.

Significantly at least twenty-five of the one hundred and fifty Psalms in *Le Livre d'Or*, the *'Book of Gold'* (i.e. one in six)

---

2 The Greek Magical Papyri in Translation, Betz (ed), 1996:26.
3 The Gospel of the Savior: An Analysis of P.Oxy.840 And Its Place in the Gospel Traditions of Early Christianity, Kruger, 2005:29.

have uses which seem to be derived from the published eighteenth century version of *Sepher Shimmush Tehillim*, indicating it was a major influence on it.

From their early Jewish and Christian roots of magical use, the Psalms would spread across the whole of Europe, as far north as the Scandinavian countries and as far east as Russia, becoming a part of local folk magic and also permeating the grimoires. The grimoires are books of magical practices with lists of spirits and/or practices and charms, which were normally hand-copied, and span the period from the thirteenth-eighteenth century. The level of Psalm usage in such grimoires as the *Key of Solomon*, the *Goetia* and the *Abramelin* show how effective the magic of these words was believed to be. Conversely, words used in conjurations in early grimoires such as *Liber Juratus,* the *Heptameron* and the *Steganographia* are found in *Le Livre d'Or*, suggesting a grimoire influence on some of the material within.

The use of Psalms in cures also occurred through both the Church and the tradition of Cunning-folk which flourished from the late Middle Ages through to the twentieth century. Another popular use amongst both Church and Cunning-folk was for protection from witchcraft and evil occurrences.

Divinatory Psalters containing the Psalms were well documented in the Slavic countries from the eleventh century onwards, a testament to the popular bibliomantic use of the Psalms. Another popular technique from the thirteenth century onwards was to make a spiral of the numbers 1-150 and throw a seed or pebble on and see which number it covered.[4]

However it was not just for divination and healing that the Psalms were employed. This work is centred on the *Livre d'Or*, a late seventeenth century French MS which was attached to a copy of the *Key of Solomon* (*Lansdowne MS 1202*), emphasising the connection between the two. As the subtitle indicates, the Psalms are those of David, and for this reason we have not included the other Psalms found in the books of *Samuel* and *Jonah*, or the additional Apocryphal Psalms found in the *Dead Sea Scrolls*.

By looking at the different intended purposes in the MS, we immediately see which uses were most popular. These were generally mundane and connected with achieving tangible results, not at all connected with any spiritual benefits. Thus the most common uses were types of protection (40), healing and health issues (27), gaining high friendships or influencing those in positions of authority (18), improving luck or fortune (15), and love magic (14). There were also significant numbers of charms for release from prison, or its opposite of detaining a person in prison (9), and to kill or destroy enemies (8), showing that it was not all benevolent and that there was a distinctly malefic streak in some of these charms.

The reputation of the Psalms for destruction is well documented, with examples going back to the third century CE. A nineteenth century description of the magical contest between the druids and Saints Patrick and Benin in 433 CE in Ireland describes them using Psalms, illustrating the popularity of such ideas:

> *"So saying, the Chief Druid set fire to the pile, and,*

---

4 Magic in Slavia Orthodoxa: The Written Tradition, Mathiesen, 1995:165.

*accompanied by two other Druids and some guards, proceeded till he came to where the saint and his assistants, in their white robes, were chanting their psalms. 'What mean these incantations?' tried the Druid".*[5]

Verses from the Psalms are found throughout the grimoires, where the efficacy of their words was not doubted. Verses from Psalms were chosen for use based on the appropriate nature of the words in them, and it is clear that the whole of the *Book of Psalms* was viewed as a book of magical power. Indeed some sources required the reading of the whole of the *Book of Psalms*, with the *Abramelin* recommending they be read in full at least twice a week.[6]

In more recent centuries the Psalms have also spread into more contemporary traditions like Dutch Pow Wow and the Diaspora of African traditions. These uses are outside the scope of this current volume, and would require substantial treatments of their own.

Of the 179 charms contained in this work, a wide range of materials were used as the basis of the charm. Paper and similar substances such as vellum and parchment predominate (61), with a high number of glass plates (8) and cooking pots (4) being the next most common. Both of these latter items recall the use of such items in ancient spells.

Certain substance dominate the list of consecrating ingredients, specifically water (30) and types of oil (22), as well as fragrant substances such as aloe wood (8) and mastic (15). The darker nature of some of the charms is also seen in the range of types of blood used, showing all of the classic animal bloods associated with the grimoires, such as white cockerel, black hen, bat, dove and goat. Interestingly there

---

5 Legendary Fictions of the Celts, Kennedy, 1891.
6 The Book of Abramelin, Worms, Dehn & Guth, 2006:129.

is also a charm which makes use of menstrual blood, which has commonly been seen as a taboo substance.

The characters used with many of the Psalms are as eclectic as the charms, being drawn from magical alphabets like Malachim Script and a mixture of hermetic and alchemical sigils.

What is clear about the uses in this extraordinary work is that they emphasise establishing harmony and success in the material world, and largely ignore the spiritual. The practices remind us of the need for magick to create effective change to be worthwhile, and through doing so then perhaps opening the practitioner up to a higher goal.

The Psalms contain a great deal of wisdom and beauty, and have been the basis of a huge range of charms and spells. Therein lies both their appeal and their power, which will be evident to the reader as they work through this unique manuscript.


*David Rankine*

Powys, Wales, April 2010

# EDITORS NOTES

Due to the poor reproduction of the characters from the MS in the electronic copy, it was necessary to hand copy the characters from the original for use in this work. Four people have checked these characters to ensure they are as close to a perfect copy of the original characters as can be achieved. A brief glance at the image quality in the following page from the original clearly shows the problem we faced with the characters which made hand copying the only option.

For all the verses, the English translation of the Latin heading is included at the beginning of the Commentary. Where the text says *"The Moon and hour as above"*, the reader should refer back through the previous Psalms until they find a reference to the Moon sign and planetary hour. A table of the planetary hours is included as Appendix 6.

Where there is reference to verses of the Psalms being used on Pentacles from copies of the grimoires known as the *Key of Solomon*, the reader is referred to *Appendix 4* or *Appendix 5*, for easy reference to their appropriate locations in readily available printed works.

Reference is made in the text to *Liber Juratus* (13th-14th century), the *Heptameron* (14th century), *Munich CLM 849* (15th century), the *Abramelin* (15th century), the *Steganographia* (early 17th century), the *Goetia* (17th century), and the *Key of Solomon* (15th-18th century). These are all grimoires, i.e. books of magical practices, which have been highly influential on the development of modern magic. *A Collection of Magical Secrets* and *A Treatise of Mixed Cabalah* are both 18th century works which resemble a Book of Secrets, i.e. collections of simple charms to achieve magical effects.

# LE LIVRE D'OR.

Touchant les Vertus & les Caracteres des Pseaumes du Prophête DAVID.

## Pseaume P.

### Beatus Vir qui non abiit.   A. Let.

Ecrivés ce Pseaume jusques à Et folium ejus non defluet avec les caracteres et le lié au bras droit d'une femme qui sera en danger de perdre son fruit et parfumés avec du Mastic, elle retiendra son fruit. El. H.H. AD. [characters] La Lune étant en Ton en X heure de 4.

### Prieres

Rendés nous Ô Seigneur aussi fertile qu'un arbre très-fructueux devant votre Divine Gloire afin qu'étant cultivés dans le nombre de vos plantes nous puissions meriter de vous plaire comme un fruit très excellent dans Sa fécondité par Notre Seigneur Jesus Christ. Amen.

### Pseaume 2.

#### Quam fremuerunt Gentes,

Si quelqu'un se sent incommodé de répétition qu'il lise ce Pseaume jusques à Hodie genui te... lui de l'huile pure

The first page of Le Livre d'Or,
being folio 91 of Lansdowne MS 1202

# THE MANUSCRIPT

Le Livre d'Or (*The Book of Gold*) comprises fo.91-114 of Lansdowne MS 1202, numbered as pages 179-230. The page numbers are included in the text in square brackets to show textual flow. The first and largest section of the manuscript is a *Key of Solomon* from the Armadel Text-Group.[7] The British Library describes this manuscript as:

"*Lansdowne 1202 4to. Les vraies Clavicules du Roi Salomon. Par Armadel. This book is elegantly written in a modern French hand, and ornamented with neat drawings of numerous talismans and other implements used in the practice of Magick, of which art this seems to be a very complete treatise. At fo. 179 is another work, entitled 'Le Livre d'Or, touchant les vertus & les caracteres des Poeaumes du Prophete David,' concluding with the Athanasian Creed.*"

The Psalm translation we have used is the Challoner revision of the Douay English translation of the Latin Vulgate Book of Psalms. The Psalm numeration in *Livre d'Or* is based on the Greek (Septuagint), and a table is included below to show the difference to the Hebrew (Masoretic) numbering:

| Greek | Hebrew | Difference |
|---|---|---|
| 1-8 | 1-8 | None |
| 9 | 9+10 | Split |
| 10-112 | 11-113 | +1 |
| 113 | 114+115 | +1 and Split |
| 114+115 | 116 | +1 and Merged |
| 116-145 | 117-146 | +1 |
| 146+147 | 147 | +1 and Merged |
| 148-150 | 148-150 | None |

---

7 See The Veritable Key of Solomon, Skinner & Rankine, 2008:30.

# LE LIVRE D'OR

*Touchant les Vertus & les Caracteres des Pseaumes du Prophête David*

# THE BOOK OF GOLD

*concerning the Qualities and Characteristics of the Psalms of the Prophet David*

# FIRST PSALM

### Beatus Vir qui non abiit. A. Let

Write this Psalm until **Et folium ejus non defluet** with the characters and the letters and bind them to the right arm of a woman who may be in danger of losing her fruit[8] and perfume with mastic and she will retain her

fruit. **El HH.AD**

. The Moon being in ♂ or in ♓ hour of ♃

## PRAYERS

Render us, oh Lord, as fertile as a fruit-laden tree before Thy divine glory, so that being cultivated amongst the multitude of Thy plants, we may be worthy and pleasing unto Thee as a most excellent fruit in its fecundity through our Lord Jesus Christ. **Amen**.

---

8 Pregnancy.

## COMMENTARY:

The Latin is the first part of verse one and reads, *"Blessed is the man who hath not walked"*.

The Mars character is an error, as the Moon could not be in Mars (another planet), and there should be a zodiacal sign here. Two possible candidates are the signs ruled by Mars, i.e. Aries or Scorpio. However the shape of the Mars symbol with the upward right pointing arrow is similar to that of the sign of Sagittarius, which is the most popular sign in this grimoire for the Moon to be in.

The binding to the right arm reflects the use of the phylactery bound to the left arm in Orthodox Judaism.

This is the same use of this Psalm as is found in *Sepher Shimmush Tehillim*. One noteworthy difference however is the use in the former of the Divine Name El Chad (AL ChD, *'Great, Strong and Only God'*), which has been corrupted to El HH.AD in this text.[9] The charm is written on deer skin, which may be derived from the earlier use on gazelle skin found in the *Cambridge Genizah*.

An early example of this protective use is also seen in the *Cambridge Genizah* T-S Ar.1.c.15 with the Psalm being written on a piece of gazelle skin parchment and bound to the pregnant woman as an amulet.[10] T-S Ar.43.200 from the same collection has a similar use of this Psalm.[11]

---

9 The Sixth and Seventh Books of Moses, Peterson, 2008:173.
10 Arabic and Judeo-Arabic Manuscripts in the Cambridge Genizah Collections, Baker & Polliack, 2001:21.
11 A Time to be Born: Customs and Folklore of Jewish Birth, Klein, 1998:111.

# PSALM 2

## *Quam fremuerunt Gentes*

*If someone feels himself to be discomposed through gastronomic repletion, he should read this Psalm until **Hodie genui te** over pure oil [180] and let the sick man be anointed by this oil and he will be cured and in order to be welcomed by a Prince, write these characters on a new tablet, wash them with the aforementioned oil and anoint your face with it and you will be welcomed. If you wish to break an earthenware vessel, write this Psalm on a new tile until **Vos figuli confringes vos**[12] and throw it onto a plate, you will be surprised at what will happen.*

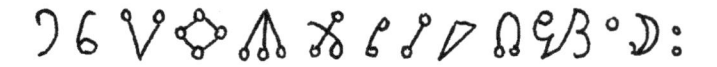

*The Moon and hour as above.*

---

## COMMENTARY:

The Latin heading is the beginning of verse one, and reads *"Why have the nations raged?"*

This Psalm also has a healing use in *Sepher Shimmush Tehillim*, being used for curing raging headaches. Verses one to eight are written on parchment with the divine name

---

12 The text has become corrupted in copying here, as the Psalm should read 'vas figuli confringes eos'.

Shaddai (ShDI, 'Almighty'), and hung around the patient's neck, and the Psalm then prayed over him.[13]

Another use in the same text is to dispel storms at sea, with the Psalm being recited, followed by meditation on the divine name Shaddai. These are then all written on a pot fragment and thrown into the sea with a prayer.[14]

Being welcomed by a prince is attributed to verses seven and eight of this Psalm, *"The Lord hath said to me: Thou art my son, this day have I begotten thee. Ask of me, and I will give thee the Gentiles for thy inheritance, and the utmost parts of the earth for thy possession"*, in *A Treatise of Mixed Cabalah.*[15]

Psalm 2 is the first of the sequence of five Psalms (2, 53, 50, 46, 67) given in the *Key of Solomon* to be recited before or during the creation of the magic circle.[16] It is also the first in the sequence of three Psalms (2, 66, 53) to be spoken on entering a room or outdoor space for a ceremony before taking any action.[17]

13 The Sixth and Seventh Books of Moses, Peterson, 2008:174.
14 Ibid, Peterson, 2008:174.
15 A Collection of Magical Secrets, Skinner, Rankine & Barron, 2009:110.
16 The Veritable Key of Solomon, Skinner & Rankine, 2009:286.
17 Ibid, 2009:342.

# PSALM 3

## *Domine quid multiplicati sunt*

*If someone has a headache, let him write this Psalm until **Et exaltans Caput meum** with the characters below and tie them around the head of the sick man and he will be healed.*

$$V \dagger \text{ⓕ} \text{ⓦ} 7 X \text{ʊ} 6 \text{Ⓙ} \text{Ⴏ} 8 \text{Ʒ} \text{ⓖ} \text{⚕} 9 X 5 \text{ꝗ} 6 \text{ı} \text{ꝺ} \text{⚕⚕} \text{ℒ} \text{Ꝺ} \text{ꝺꝺ} \text{ꝝ}$$

*The Moon as above.*

## ORATION

*Pour upon us, Oh Lord, Thine Holy Blessing, so that being upheld by Thy mercy, we will not fear any traps laid for us by our enemies nor will we be afraid of their great number, which doth assail us. By our Lord Jesus Christ, so may it be.*

## COMMENTARY:

The Latin heading is the first half of verse two, *"Why, O Lord, are they multiplied that afflict me?"*

This Psalm is also used for healing in *Sepher Shimmush Tehillim*, for curing severe headaches and backaches. The Psalm and the divine name Adon (ADVN, *'Lord'*) are recited over olive oil and the oil anointed onto the head.[18]

This is the first Psalm in the sequence of seven (3, 8, 30, 41, 59, 50, 129) for use in the preparation of the needle, burin and other iron instruments in the *Key of Solomon*.[19]

In the *Goetia*, the first of the Shemhamphorash angels, Vehuiah, is associated with verse four of this Psalm, *"But thou, O Lord art my protector, my glory, and the lifter up of my head"*.[20]

Verses six and seven, *"I have slept and taken my rest: and I have risen up, because the Lord hath protected me. I will not fear thousands of the people, surrounding me: arise, O Lord; save me, O my God"*, are given in *A Collection of Magical Secrets* for resisting domestic enemies.[21]

---

18 The Sixth and Seventh Books of Moses, Peterson, 2008:175.
19 The Key of Solomon the King, Mathers, 1976:115.
20 The Goetia of Dr Rudd, Skinner & Rankine, 2007:408.
21 A Collection of Magical Secrets, Skinner, Rankine & Barron, 2009:83.

# PSALM 4

## *Cum invocarem exaudivit me Deus*

*It relieves the following afflictions, of which Saint Cassiodorus both confirms and affirms [181] and he who says it in a devoted manner, will be delivered from all watery perils and from all accidents.*
*It is also useful for obtaining the friendship of great people. You should rise with the Sun on a Thursday and recite it 7 times with the name of the Intelligence and have the characters written on your left hand and just before speaking to the person, he should speak the name of the Intelligence and stare at the characters on his hand – speak with confidence.*

**Intelligence Ha Character**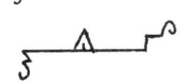

## COMMENTARY:

The Latin heading is the first part of verse two, *"When I called upon him, the God of my justice heard me"*.

The name Ha occurs in conjurations in the *Heptameron*, and it is clear that here it is used as the name of the intelligence (spirit).

One of the uses given for this Psalm in *Sepher Shimmush Tehillim* is for the success of a cause before magistrates or princes, for which it is to be recited seven times before sunrise with an appropriate prayer. Another use in the same text is to reverse misfortune, by reciting the Psalm three times before sunrise and then meditating on the divine name Yihehyeh (IHHI, *'He is and will be'*).[22]

This Psalm is also used *'To receive affection from kings and other great people'* by reciting it over rose oil and then rubbing the oil three times in the face before going to meet the person in question.[23]

Saint Cassiodorus was a Roman monk and writer (c.490-583CE), who originally held high office as a senator. His writings were significant both in espousing an intellectual approach to scripture and also for preserving otherwise lost knowledge on musical theory applied to the use of voice and instrument in services. His most noted writings were on the Psalms, and he also had the distinction of creating the template for subsequent Western monasteries, the one he created being the first (in the West).

---

22 The Sixth and Seventh Books of Moses, Peterson, 2008:175.
23 A Collection of Magical Secrets, Skinner, Rankine & Barron, 2009:83.

# PSALM 5

## *Verba mea auribus percipe Domine*

*This Psalm is used against tempters, liars, perjurers and for the souls of the dead.*

*In addition, it is good for locations or places that are being besieged and is also good for obtaining the friendship of great Lords. St Jerôme says that it is good for important things to the soul and when it is said with contrition, you will obtain from God all the things that you ask of Him.*

*In order to make this work, you should take some olive oil, over which you recite this Psalm 3 times then rub this oil into your forehead and onto the top of your hand, onto which you will have written the name of the Intelligence, as well as the Character and you should see the resulting effects from it.* **Intelligence Canielvel Caniel, according to others Ramul.**

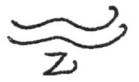

**Characters**          **according to others**

*[182]*

## COMMENTARY:

The Latin in the heading is the first part of verse two, *"Give ear, O Lord, to my words"*.

Another use whose origins are drawn from *Sepher Shimmush Tehillim*, where the Psalm is said three times over pure olive oil and anointed onto the face, hands and feet, with the divine name Chananyah (ChNNIH, *'Merciful God'*) for the success of a cause before magistrates or princes.[24]

The names Canielvel and Ramul do not seem to occur elsewhere, but Caniel is first found in the *Steganographia* of Trithemius as one of the aerial spirits serving the Prince Barmiel.[25]

St Jerome (sometimes spelled as St Hierom) was born in 347 CE in Stridon, now located in modern-day Croatia. He was a Christian priest and an apologist, many of his works vehemently attacking opposers of Christian Orthodoxy but is best known for his new translation of the Bible into Latin, much of which would later become part of the Latin Vulgate Bible. He also revised the Psalter. It is said that many of his commentaries on the Scriptures aligned closely with commentaries from Jewish Tradition. He died in 420 CE.

The Palermo ring, a seventh century gold ring for protecting a married couple, contains the second half of verse thirteen, *"thou hast crowned us, as with a shield of thy good will"*.[26] This is not an isolated example, with another such ring being held in Russia.[27]

The second half of verse five, first half of verse six and second half of verse seven are connected to be used for throwing lying or treacherous men off your scent in *A*

---

24 The Sixth and Seventh Books of Moses, Peterson, 2008:176.
25 The Steganographia of Trithemius, McLean (ed), 1982:33.

26 Art, Medicine and Magic in Early Byzantium, Vikan, 1984:83.
27 Byzantine Art in the Collections of the USSR, Banck, ND, 106c.

*Collection of Magical Scents.* The resulting expression is, *"because thou art not a God that willest iniquity. Neither shall the wicked dwell near thee: Thou wilt destroy all that speak a lie. The bloody and the deceitful man the Lord will abhor".*[28]

---

28 A Collection of Magical Secrets, Skinner, Rankine & Barron, 2009:112.

# PSALM 6

## *Domine ne in furore tuo arguas me*

*This is good for consoling the sinner and to remove from him the grief of having offended God and this makes him look into his heart. Saint Cassiodorus says that whoever recites it piously seven times in a row, will change the evil will of an ungodly Judge and will prevent him from condemning him unjustly.*

*It is good for all the labours and torments of the Spirit, reciting it seven times and with each time speak the name of the Intelligence and the immediately say; Here I pray to Thee, Lord of Salvation through the Holy Names of this Psalm, that Thou mayest deliver me from (such a torment or such an ill), from which Thou canst deliver those who are pleasing unto Thee.*

*It is also good for sick people, who have diseased eyes. It should be recited it seven times for three days consecutively along with the name of the Intelligence and for each time you recite the Psalm, write its name and its character on a lettuce leaf and you should touch your eyes with it.*

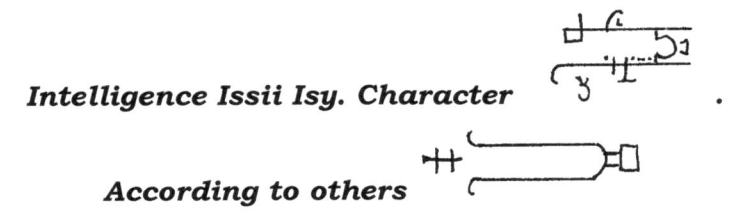

***Intelligence Issii Isy. Character***

***According to others***

## COMMENTARY:

The Latin in the heading is the first part of verse two, *"O Lord, rebuke me not in thy indignation."* The names Issii and Isy given to the intelligence (spirit) do not occur in other grimoires.

This is the first of the seven Penitential Psalms, which are found in the fifteenth century *Abramelin* and were also used by Dr John Dee in the late sixteenth century. These Psalms were sometimes given as part of the process as purificatory preparation for evocation in the grimoires.

One use given in *Sepher Shimmush Tehillim* matches the final use here, which is for healing diseased eyes by saying the prescribed prayer (given in the book) seven times after reciting the Psalm with the name Yeshayah (IShAIH, *'Help is with the Lord')*, over a period of three days.[29] Another use in the same work is to recite the Psalm seven times with a prayer for protection from dangers by land or sea.

In the *Goetia*, two of the Shemhamphorash angels are associated with this Psalm, the fourth, Elemiah with verse five, *"Turn to me, O Lord, and deliver my soul: O save me for thy mercy's sake"*,[30] and the fifty-eighth, Yeialel, with verse four *"And my soul is troubled exceedingly: but thou, O Lord, how long?"*[31]

---

29 The Sixth and Seventh Books of Moses, Peterson, 2008:177.
30 The Goetia of Dr Rudd, Skinner & Rankine, 2007:408.
31 Ibid, 2007:411.

# PSALM 7

*Domine Deus meus in te speravi, salvum me fac*

*It procures the assistance of God if you say it piously when in times of need, according to St. Jerôme; it also procures relief for prisoners and in the same way it prevents you from being cheated [183] by whomever and it serves against enemies and against lawsuits, if you carry it upon yourself along with its character and its Intelligence and if you are pursued from the rear, take some earth and recite this Psalm over it and write the character and the Intelligence on it and then throw this powder along with what you have written into it, into the face of your enemies and they will retreat.*

*If you have any specific enemies, take an earthenware vase and fill it with water from a spring or from a river and recite from this verse in the Psalm four times*
**Exurge Domine in ira tua** *until the end of this Psalm and then add to it, My God, strike down mine enemies to my feet and trample upon them, as Thou didst bring down the house of* **Abraham** *and may they flee from before me.*

*Then throw this water onto the place over which your enemies will pass and you will always vanquish them.*

*If you involved in a lawsuit, while going before the judge, repeat the name of the Intelligence and you will*

*find favour:* **Intelligence Eliel. Characters** 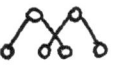 .

## COMMENTARY:

The Latin in the heading is the first half of verse two, *"O Lord my God, in thee have I put my trust: save me"*. Eliel is a spirit serving under the Prince Maseriel in the *Steganographia*.[32] The uses found here are the same as in *Sepher Shimmush Tehillim*, even down to the throwing of earth, clearly show this was the likely source. The divine name used is El Elion (AL, ALIVN, *'Most High God'*).[33] The same work also recommends reciting the Psalm with a prayer to El Elion before appearing in front of a judge.

It is the fourth of five Psalms used for preparing the holy drink against elf influence and the devil's temptations in the Anglo-Saxon *Lacnunga* MS (C10th-11th CE).[34]

In the *Goetia* verse eighteen of this Psalm, *"I will give glory to the Lord according to his justice: and will sing to the name of the Lord the most high"*, is associated with the fifty-second Shemhamphorash angel, Aumamiah.[35] This Psalm is recited before sleep as part of a rite for receiving a reply during sleep. The rite requires three days chastity and purity, and includes the inscription of a sigil and intelligence name on a laurel leaf with rose water ink.[36]

Lines based on verses of this Psalm are used in a charm in the *Abramelin*. The words *"Bad luck will fall on your head and spite cover your head"* (based on verse sixteen) are written on a lead plate after sunset, and this is fumigated whilst this prayer is repeated seven times, *"Stand up, Adonai, in your rage, and raise yourself in anger upon my enemies"* (based on verse six).[37]

---

32 The Steganographia of Trithemius, McLean, 1982:39.
33 The Sixth and Seventh Books of Moses, Peterson, 2008:177.
34 Leechcraft, Pollington, 2004:193.
35 The Goetia of Dr Rudd, Skinner & Rankine, 2007:411.
36 A Collection of Magical Secrets, Skinner, Rankine & Barron, 2009:53.
37 The Book of Abramelin, Worms, Dehn & Guth, 2006:51.

# PSALM 8

### *Domine Dominus Noster*

*In order to prevent children crying and in order to hold honey bees, write this Psalm and attach it to the right arm of the child and he will cry no longer and in order to take the bees, if you recite the first verse only from this Psalm, you will be able to carry them [184] to their territory.*

*The Moon being in* ♂ *or in* ♉ *hour of the* ☉

## ORATION

*Oh Almighty God, we pray to Thy praiseworthy name most humbly, with the wish to make us worthy of the duties of servitude, which we owe to Thee and in this way, Thou hast created and formed all creatures to the use of mankind through our Lord Jesus Christ, so may it be.*

## COMMENTARY:

The Latin in the heading is the first few words of verse two, *"O Lord our Lord"*.

Again the Mars character is an error, as the Moon could not be in Mars (another planet), and there should be a zodiacal sign here. As discussed in Psalm 1, the most likely candidates are either Sagittarius or possibly the signs ruled by Mars, i.e. Aries or Scorpio.

The reference to bees is significant in that they are needed by the magician as a source of virgin wax for making pentacles.

In *Sepher Shimmush Tehillim* this Psalm is used to gain the goodwill of men in business transactions. This is done by reciting the Psalm whilst thinking of the divine name Rachmiel (RChMIAL, *'God of Compassion or Mercy'*) for three days after sunset. The associated prayer is said three times over olive oil and the face, hands and feet anointed with it.[38]

This Psalm is the first in the sequence of eight Psalms (8, 21, 27, 29, 32, 51, 72, 134) to be recited during the consecration of the Pentacles in the *Key of Solomon*. The Pentacle is held over the incense towards the rising sun and the Psalms recited with devotion.[39]

This Psalm is one of those in the sequence of nineteen (130, 14, 101, 8, 83, 67, 71, 132, 112, 125, 45, 46, 21, 50, 129, 138, 48, 109, 52) recited for conjuration of the wax used in making the Pentacles in the *Key of Solomon*.[40]

This is the second Psalm in the sequence of seven (3, 8, 30, 41, 59, 50, 129) for use in the preparation of the needle, burin and other iron instruments in the *Key of Solomon*.[41]

In the *Goetia*, the first half of verse two, *"O Lord our Lord, how admirable is thy name in the whole earth"* of this Psalm is associated with the seventeenth Shemhamphorash angel, Lauviah.[42]

This Psalm is the first of two used in a technique of seeking answers from the appropriate planetary archangel of the day.[43]

---

38 The Sixth and Seventh Books of Moses, Peterson, 2008:179.
39 The Veritable Key of Solomon, Skinner & Rankine, 2008:304.
40 The Key of Solomon the King, Mathers, 1976:114.
41 Ibid, 1976:115.
42 The Goetia of Dr Rudd, Skinner & Rankine, 2007:409.
43 A Collection of Magical Secrets, Skinner, Rankine & Barron, 2009:97-8.

# PSALM 9

### *Confitebor tibi Domine. Eehie*

*If you wish to be honoured by your King or Prince, write all of this Psalm onto a glass plate with the characters below in the Name of Jesus Christ and of St Etienne,[44] wash all of it with olive oil and then rub your face with it.*

*. The Moon as above.*

## ORATION

*Lend, Oh God, Thy holy ear to our confession, Thou who hast never abandoned those who are penitent, so that being delivered from the Gates of Death, we may avoid the traps that have been laid for us. Through Our Lord Jesus Christ.[45] So mote it be.*

---

44 St. Etienne is the French version of St Stephen.
45 The text gives NSJC, a contraction of Notre Sauveur Jesus Christ.

## COMMENTARY:

The Latin in the heading is the first part of verse two, *"I will give praise to thee, O Lord"*. The divine name in the heading is clearly a miscopied version of Eheieh (AHIH, *'I am'*, the divine name of the Sephira of Kether on the Qabalistic Tree of Life).

St Stephen is venerated as a Saint in many Christian traditions and was one of the first Saints in the early church to bear the title Archdeacon. There is no record of his birth, but he died circa 35 CE in Jerusalem, when he had been tried for blasphemy against Moses and God and was stoned to death (*Acts 6:11*).

To exorcise a demon, this Psalm was whispered nine times with its associated mystical names over a new pot filled with freshly drawn water with some olive oil poured in. The liquid was then used to bathe the victim.[46]

*Sepher Shimmush Tehillim* gives two different uses for this Psalm. The first use is for restoring sick male children to health, writing the Psalm on new parchment and hanging it around the boy's neck with a prayer whilst thinking of the divine name Eheieh Asher Eheieh (AHIH, AShR AHH, *'I am that I am'*, often used for the Sephira of Kether in the Qabalah).[47] The second use is against the ill-will and power of enemies, reciting the Psalm with another prayer which contains the same divine name.[48]

This is the point where the Septuagint and Masoretic Psalms diverge. Thus the Psalm attributions in the *Sepher Shimmush Tehillim* from this point are one greater than those in *Le Livre d'Or*. For this reason there is another attributed Psalm following this paragraph, and the subsequent Psalms

---

46 Jewish Magic and Superstition, Trachtenberg, 1939:160.
47 The Sixth and Seventh Books of Moses, Peterson, 2008:179.
48 Ibid, Peterson, 2008:179.

as far as 146 will be matched on their content rather than the number which is out by one.

In *Sepher Shimmush Tehillim* this Psalm is used for banishing unclean, evil or restless spirits. Spring water is gathered in an earthenware pot in the name of the patient, and olive oil added whilst the divine name El Mez (AL MZ, *'Strong God of the Oppressed'*) is kept in mind. The Psalm is recited nine times with a prayer at the end of each recital.[49]

In the *Goetia*, four of the Shemhamphorash angels are associated with verses of this Psalm. The sixth angel Lelahel is associated with verse eleven, *"Sing ye to the Lord, who dwelleth in Sion: declare his ways among the Gentiles"*;[50] the twelfth Shemhamphorash angel, Hahaiah, is associated with verse twenty-one, *"Why, O Lord, hast thou retired afar off? Why dost thou slight us in our wants, in the time of trouble"*;[51] the fourteenth angel Mebahel with verse nine *"And the Lord is become a refuge for the poor: a helper in due time in tribulation"*;[52] and the twenty-fifth angel Nithahaiah with verse two *"I will give praise to thee, O Lord, with my whole heart: I will relate all thy wonders"*.[53]

Verses fifteen and sixteen, *"the Gentiles have stuck fast in the destruction which they have prepared. Their foot hath been taken in the very snare which they hid. The Lord shall be known when he executeth judgments: the sinner hath been caught in the works of his own hands"*, are given in order to recover hidden objects in *A Treatise of Mixed Cabalah*.[54]

---

49 Ibid, Peterson, 2008:179.
50 The Goetia of Dr Rudd, Skinner & Rankine, 2007:408.
51 Ibid, 2007:408.
52 Ibid, 2007:408.
53 Ibid, 2007:409.
54 A Collection of Magical Secrets, Skinner, Rankine & Barron, 2009:112.

# PSALM 10

### *In te Domine confido. Elmas*

*Write this Psalm on a parchment of wild billy-goat until*
**Ignis & sulphur & Spiritus procellarum** *and also
the [185] characters with a pen from bronze and bury it
under the door of your enemies. Write in the same way
on another piece or parchment and place it upon the
head of a dead man; if your enemy is a man, bury it in
the sepulchre of a woman and if it is a woman, in that of
a man and may the death take place within a day.*

*The Moon being in ♂ or in ♍ hour of ♃ or of ♀.*

## ORATION

*Cast Thine merciful eyes, Oh Lord, upon us, who are
beaten down by our poverty; cover us with the arch of
our faith, so that being sheltered from injury of unjust
blood, we may serve Thee and preserve justice through
our Lord Jesus Christ. So mote it be.*

## COMMENTARY:

The Latin in the title is the opening words of verse two, *"In the Lord I put my trust"*.

For the third time the Mars character is given in error, as the Moon could not be in Mars (another planet), and there should be a zodiacal sign here. As discussed in the commentary to Psalm 1, the most likely candidates are either Sagittarius or possibly the signs ruled by Mars, i.e. Aries or Scorpio.

The bronze pen is reminiscent of spells in the *Greek Magical Papyri* (C2nd BCE – C5th CE).

This is a similarity to *Sepher Shimmush Tehillim* in that the charm for the Psalm given there is used for protection from persecution, with the divine name Pele (PLA, *'Wonderful'*).[55]

In *A Treatise of Mixed Cabalah*, verses three and eight are combined in a charm, *"For, lo, the wicked have bent their bow; they have prepared their arrows in the quiver; to shoot in the dark the upright of heart. For the Lord is just, and hath loved justice: his countenance hath beheld righteousness"*, to save yourself from pirates and assassins.[56]

---

55 The Sixth and Seventh Books of Moses, Peterson, 2008:180.
56 A Collection of Magical Secrets, Skinner, Rankine & Barron, 2009:118.

# PSALM 11

## *Salvum me fac Domine*

*If you have an enemy who says something evil about you, in order to prevent him from doing so, write this Psalm and the characters on a glass plate, perfume it with borax, read the entire Psalm over water and bury the plate under the door of your enemy.*

*The Moon being as above.*

## ORATION

*Have compassion on our fragility O Father most Holy, give to us [186] the grace to be able to please you with a glad heart and protect us from the mouths of those who speak much ill of me. Through our Lord Jesus Christ, So mote it be.*

## COMMENTARY:

The Latin in the title is the opening words of verse two, *"Save me, O Lord"*.

As with the previous verse, in *Sepher Shimmush Tehillim*

this Psalm is used for protection from persecution. The holy name used therein with this Psalm is Aviel (AVIAL, *'Strong God, My Father'*).[57]

In *A Treatise of Mixed Cabalah*, verse six, *"By reason of the misery of the needy, and the groans of the poor, now will I arise, saith the Lord. I win set him in safety; I will deal confidently in his regard"*, is suggested to deliver a sick man from all infirmity.[58]

57 The Sixth and Seventh Books of Moses, Peterson, 2008:180.
58 A Collection of Magical Secrets, Skinner, Rankine & Barron, 2009:120.

# PSALM 12

## *Usquequo Domine oblivisceris me in fine? Ja*

*Against rogues and for teaching children easily.
If you are afraid that rogues may set a trap for you,
recite this Psalm three times and they will flee. If you
have fallen asleep in a desert, read this Psalm until **ne
quando dicat** three times and with the aid of God, you
will have naught to fear. If you wish to make a child
more amenable to Education, write these characters,
wash them with holy water, which you then collect in a
drinking glass and give it to the child to drink. He will
have an amazing idea*

*The Moon being in ♂ or ♊ hour of ♃ or ♀.*

## ORATION

*Turn not Thine face away from us, Oh Lord, Almighty
God, for fear that our enemies may prevail against us;
disperse rather their evil intention of heart, through
Thine aid, so that we may obtain an easy death through
our Lord Jesus Christ. So mote it be.*

*[187]*

## COMMENTARY:

The Latin in the title is from verse one, *"How long, O Lord, wilt thou forget me unto the end?"* Ja occurs in the *Heptameron* as a divine name, and may be a contraction of Yah.

Once more the Mars character is an error, as the Moon could not be in Mars (another planet), and there should be a zodiacal sign here. As discussed in the commentary to Psalm 1, the most likely candidates are either Sagittarius or possibly the signs ruled by Mars, i.e. Aries or Scorpio.

In *Sepher Shimmush Tehillim* this Psalm is given for protection from unnatural death and all bodily sufferings for twenty-four hours. The Psalm is recited with devotion whilst thinking of the divine name Esriel (ASRIAL, *'My help is the Mighty God'*) and the appropriate prayer.[59] The same prayer and Psalm are also given for speaking over a plate which heals eye conditions.

Verses 4-5, *"Enlighten my eyes that I never sleep in death: lest at any time my enemy say: I have prevailed against him"* is written around the edge of a Solar Pentacle (see Sun 4, Appendix 4) to make spirits appear visibly, and not be able to be invisible. A Saturnian Pentacle against sudden death and accidents also uses the same verses around the edge (see Saturn 8, Appendix 5), as does a Jupiterian Pentacle for games of chance (see Jupiter 1, Appendix 5).

This Psalm is used as part of the preparation of the Wonderful Ring of Lucibel (Lucifer) in *A Collection of Magical Secrets*.[60] In *A Treatise of Mixed Cabalah*, verses four and five, *"Consider, and hear me, O Lord my God. Enlighten my*

---

59 The Sixth and Seventh Books of Moses, Peterson, 2008:180.
60 A Collection of Magical Secrets, Skinner, Rankine & Barron, 2009:75-7.

*eyes that I never sleep in death: lest at any time my enemy say: I have prevailed against him. They that trouble me will rejoice when I am moved"*, are given to save yourself from pirates and assassins.[61]

---

# PSALM 13

*Dixit incipiens in corde suo. Non est Deus. El.*

*If you want to appear Majestic before someone and be respected for it, read this Psalm over pure water until* **Quoniam Dominus in generatione Justa est** *and write the characters and perfume it with mastic and musk and wash over them with pure water and pour it out before the door of the person, by whom you wish to*

*be respected*

*The Moon as above.*

## COMMENTARY:

The Latin in the title is from verse one, *"The fool hath said in his heart: There is no God"*. El, meaning *'God'*, is the divine name of the Sephira of Chesed on the Qabalistic Tree of Life.

A similar use of this Psalm is seen in *Sepher Shimmush Tehillim,* where it is used for gaining favour, in conjunction with a prayer and the divine name El Amet (AL AMTh, *'The True God'*).[62]

A parallel may be seen in the use of this Psalm as the second in the sequence of five Psalms (17, 13, 54, 80, 117) to be recited whilst bathing before conjuration in the *Key of Solomon.*[63]

---

62 The Sixth and Seventh Books of Moses, Peterson, 2008:180.
63 The Veritable Key of Solomon, Skinner & Rankine, 2008:341.

# PSALM 14

## *Domine quis habitabit in tabernaculo tuo?*

*If you want to enter into any town or approach any Prince, read this Psalm while entering and write these characters and carry them upon you.*

*The Moon in ♂ or in Ⅱ hour of ♀ or ♃.*

---

## COMMENTARY:

The Latin in the title is from verse one, *"Lord, who shall dwell in thy tabernacle?"*

For the fifth time the Mars character is an error, as the Moon could not be in Mars (another planet), and there should be a zodiacal sign here. As discussed in the commentary to Psalm 1, the most likely candidates are either Sagittarius or possibly the signs ruled by Mars, i.e. Aries or Scorpio.

In *Sepher Shimmush Tehillim* this Psalm is used for several purposes, including protection from evil spirits, which parallels enchantments of wicked people to a degree. The Psalm is recited over a new pot filled with well water whilst contemplating the divine name Iali (ILI, *'My Lord'*). The appropriate prayer is then recited as the patient is washed with the water.[64]

This Psalm is one of those in the sequence of nineteen (130, 14, 101, 8, 83, 67, 71, 132, 112, 125, 45, 46, 21, 50, 129, 138, 48, 109, 52) recited for conjuration of the wax used in making the Pentacles in the *Key of Solomon*.[65]

---

64 The Sixth and Seventh Books of Moses, Peterson, 2008:181.
65 The Key of Solomon the King, Mathers, 1976:114.

# PSALM 15

### *Conserva me Domine, Hely*

*If you want to be protected from enchantments of wicked people and prevent them from harming you, write this Psalm and these characters and carry them with you.*

*The Moon as above.*

## COMMENTARY:

The Latin in the title is from verse one, *"Preserve me, O Lord"*. Hely, meaning *'Ascension'*, is a divine name used in a number of the grimoires including *Liber Juratus*, the *Key of Solomon* and the *Goetia*.

*Sepher Shimmush Tehillim* gives a technique for learning the name of a thief, again showing a degree of similarity. This is done by taking mud or slime and mixing it with sand, all taken from the same stream. Write the names of the suspects on strips of paper and apply the mixture on the reverse of the paper. Then lay them one by one in a large clean basin, filled with water from the same stream whilst reciting the Psalm ten times with the appropriate prayer and thinking of the divine name Chai (ChI, *'Living'*). The slip of paper with the thief's name on will rise to the surface if he is there.[66] This Psalm is also credited with turning sorrows to joys, changing enemies to friends and dispersing pain and sorrow if said on a daily basis.[67]

In the *Goetia*, the sixty-ninth Shemhamphorash angel Rahel is associated with verse five of this Psalm, *"The Lord is the portion of my inheritance and of my cup: it is thou that wilt restore my inheritance to me".*[68]

Verses five and six, *"The Lord is the portion of my inheritance and of my cup: it is thou that wilt restore my inheritance to me. The lines are fallen unto me in goodly places: for my inheritance is goodly to me",* are used in *A Treatise of Mixed Cabalah* to prosper in all things.[69]

---

66 The Sixth and Seventh Books of Moses, Peterson, 2008:181.
67 Ibid, Peterson, 2008:181.
68 The Goetia of Dr Rudd, Skinner & Rankine, 2007:412.
69 A Collection of Magical Secrets, Skinner, Rankine & Barron, 2009:112.

# PSALM 16

*Exaudi Domine justitiam meam. H Hav*

*If you wish to avoid scandal and strife, read this [188] Psalm until **Eripe amimam meam ab impio** seven times and write these characters and perfume them with mastic and carry them upon you.*

$$\forall \; \wp \; \mathcal{J}\mathcal{Y} \; \mathcal{H}\mathcal{F} \; \mathcal{F}\mathcal{L} \; \mathcal{B}\mathcal{J}\mathcal{S} \; \wedge \vee \geqslant \mathcal{C} \times \mathcal{N}$$

*. The Moon as above.*

## COMMENTARY:

The Latin in the title is from verse one, *"Hear, O Lord, my justice"*. Hav is a name used on one of the pentacles in the copy of the *Key of Solomon* to which the *Le Livre d'Or* was bound.

In *Sepher Shimmush Tehillim* this Psalm is given for recitation to protect a traveller from all evil for twenty-four hours, when recited with its appropriate prayer and the divine name Yah (IH, *'God'*, divine name of the Sephira of Chokmah in the Qabalah, and the first half of Tetragrammaton, being known as the *'Inner Chamber'*) concentrated on.[70]

---

70 The Sixth and Seventh Books of Moses, Peterson, 2008:182.

# PSALM 17

*Diligam te Domine fortitudo mea. Sad.*

*If there are any sick people in any one place, take a new
earthenware bowl and fill it with pure water and read
this Psalm over it and write these characters in the
corners of the house and they will be healed.*

*The Moon as above this one.*

## COMMENTARY:

The Latin in the title is verse two, *"I will love thee, O
Lord, my strength"*. The word Sad is probably an abbreviated
form of the divine name Shaddai (ShDI, *'Almighty'*, a divine
name attributed to the Sephira of Yesod on the Qabalistic
Tree of Life).

This technique could hint at a demonic aspect to the
sickness, as the use of bowls of water for containing demons
is well documented in Jewish lore (see Flavius Josephus and
also the *Sepher Shimmush Tehillim*).

A similar use is seen in *A Treatise of Mixed Cabalah*,
where verses five, six and thirty-six, *"The sorrows of death
surrounded me: and the torrents of iniquity troubled me. The
sorrows of hell encompassed me: and the snares of death
prevented me. And thou hast given me the protection of thy
salvation: and thy right hand hath held me up: And thy
discipline hath corrected me unto the end: and thy discipline,*

*the same shall teach me"* are given to deliver a sick man from all infirmity.[71]

In the same work, verses three and four, *"The Lord is my firmament, my refuge, and my deliverer. My God is my helper, and in him will I put my trust. My protector and the horn of my salvation, and my support. Praising I will call upon the Lord: and I shall be saved from my enemies"*, are given for use against highway robbers.[72]

In *Sepher Shimmush Tehillim* this Psalm is used for treating people close to death, through recitation over olive oil and water.[73]  The Psalm is also given in that text for protection from robbers, used with a prayer and concentrating on the divine name El Yah (EL IH, *'Mighty God'*).[74]

This Psalm is the first in the sequence of five Psalms (17, 13, 54, 80, 117) to be recited whilst bathing before conjuration in the *Key of Solomon*.[75]

Verse 8, *"The earth shook and trembled: the foundations of the mountains were troubled and were moved, because he was angry with them"* is used in a Saturnian Pentacle for creating earthquakes (see Saturn 7, Appendix 4).  A derivative version of the same Pentacle attributed to the Moon is described as preventing earthquakes (see Moon 4, Appendix 5).

In the *Goetia* the eleventh Shemhamphorash angel Lauviah is associated with verse forty-seven of this Psalm, *"The Lord liveth, and blessed be my God, and let the God of my salvation be exalted"*.[76]

---

71 A Collection of Magical Secrets, Skinner, Rankine & Barron, 2009:120.
72 Ibid, 2009:119.
73 The Sixth and Seventh Books of Moses, Peterson, 2008:182.
74 Ibid, Peterson, 2008:182.
75 The Veritable Key of Solomon, Skinner & Rankine, 2008:341.
76 The Goetia of Dr Rudd, Skinner & Rankine, 2007:408.

# PSALM 18

*Cæli enarrant gloriam Dei. El Ja.*

*Write this Psalm until **Exultavit ut gigans** and place it under the feet of a woman in labour, who cannot give birth. As soon as she does give birth, write this Psalm also onto a glass plate with the characters and perfume them with aloes and wash them with holy water and give it to her to drink and read out this Psalm and rub it onto her stomach.*

*The Moon as above.*

## COMMENTARY:

The Latin in the title is the first part of verse two, *"The heavens shew forth the glory of God"*. El Ja is probably a form of El Yah, meaning *'Lord God'*, a combination of the divine names of the Sephiroth of Chokmah and Chesed in the Qabalistic Tree of Life. However we may note that Ja also occurs in the *Heptameron* as a divine name.

This use is another one that seems to be derived from *Sepher Shimmush Tehillim* where it is recommended for a prolonged and difficult labour. The procedure is to take earth from a crossroad, write the first five verses of the Psalm on it and lay it on the abdomen of the woman. The Psalm is then recited seven times with an appropriate prayer whilst thinking of the divine name He (HI, the first two letters in the Tetragrammaton reversed) and the earth left on the woman until she has successfully given birth.[77]

Another use in this work is to bestow intelligence on a son to ensure he understands his lessons. The Psalm is placed over a cup of wine and honey, and the divine name pronounced with an appropriate prayer. The boy then drinks the wine and honey.[78] A third use is for driving away evil spirits by reciting the Psalm and prayer seven times over the afflicted person with the divine name.[79]

Verse two is used in the second of two versions of the conjuration of the Prince of the Thumb found in *Munich CLM 849*, for obtaining information. The verse, *"The heavens shew forth the glory of God, and the firmament declareth the work of his hands"*, is recited whilst casting the second of the three circles.[80]

77 The Sixth and Seventh Books of Moses, Peterson, 2008:183.
78 Ibid, Peterson, 2008:183.
79 Ibid, Peterson, 2008:183.
80 Forbidden Rites, Kieckhefer, 1997:334.

# PSALM 19

*Exaudiant te Dominus in die tribulationis. Hy.*

*If you read this Psalm three times every day, you will be blessed by the Lord and write these characters and carry them on you [189]. If you read this Psalm over a sick person; if he is to live, he will be calmer and will be at rest but if he is not to live, he will die immediately.*

The Moon as above.

## COMMENTARY:

The Latin in the title is the first half of verse two, *"May the Lord hear thee in the day of tribulation"*. Hy is a name found in conjurations in the *Heptameron* of Peter de Abano.

*Sepher Shimmush Tehillim* uses the Psalm seven times over a mixture of rose oil with water and salt. The use therein however is for remaining free from danger for a day; with a prayer and the divine name Yeho (IHV, the first three letters of Tetragrammaton, Yod, Heh, Vav).[81] It is also given for swaying a judge in your favour. This Psalm is one of those used in order to attain high honours, high rank and increase good fortune in the *Sepher Shimmush Tehillim*. The sequence is 91, 93, 22, 19, 23, 99 (see Psalm 91 for more details).[82]

---

81 The Sixth and Seventh Books of Moses, Peterson, 2008:184.
82 Ibid, Peterson, 2008:184.

In Jewish folklore this Psalm was recited nine times to a pregnant woman to help ease her birth. If this did not help it was recited another nine times, and then finally the following prayer was spoken:

*"I conjure you, Armisael, angel who governs the womb, that you help this woman and the child in her body to life and peace. Amen, Amen, Amen."*[83]

Verse six and the opening phrase of verse seven, *"We will rejoice in thy salvation; and in the name of our God we shall be exalted. The Lord fulfil all thy petitions"*, is given in *A Treatise of Mixed Cabalah* for knowing whether a sick person will die or live.[84]

83 Jewish Magic and Superstition, Trachtenberg, 1939:201-2.
84 A Collection of Magical Secrets, Skinner, Rankine & Barron, 2009:112.

# PSALM 20

## Domine in virtute tua lætabitur Rex. Jehu.

*If you wish to be welcomed by everybody, regardless of how your character or status may be, read this Psalm over rose oil seven times and write this Psalm and the characters onto a new tablet, which you will then perfume with mastic and wash with the oil from above and anoint your face with it and you will receive many honours.*

Œ Ε )ᵒ𝒯 𝓛 𝓊𝓸𝓸 ℛ, Ɛⁱ 𝓛 𝓥 ⋞ ⋞ Ε ⋞)𝒫𝒟 Ε 𝓨𝓿𝓙𝓍

*The Moon as above.*

## COMMENTARY:

The Latin in the title is the first half of verse two, *"In thy strength, O Lord, the king shall joy"*. Jehu is a divine name made of the first three letters of Tetragrammaton, Yod Heh Vav (IHV).

In *Sepher Shimmush Tehillim* this Psalm is given for safety from dangers during a storm at sea. Rose oil, water, salt and resin are mixed with the recitation of the Psalm and the divine name Yehach (IHCh, unknown meaning), and the mixture poured into the sea with an appropriate prayer. Anointing the mixture on the face is given for being received favourably by a king or other high ranking official.[85]

---

85 The Sixth and Seventh Books of Moses, Peterson, 2008:184.

An abbreviated form of this use is given in *A Treatise of Mixed Cabalah*, where verse fourteen, *"Be thou exalted, O Lord, in thy own strength: we will sing and praise thy power"*, is credited with the same ability to be welcomed by all men.[86]

---

86 A Collection of Magical Secrets, Skinner, Rankine & Barron, 2009:110.

# PSALM 21

*Deus Deus meus respice in me. Ja Het.*

*If you fall into the hands of petty people and you fear their malice, say this Psalm seven times and you will be delivered from them. Likewise, write these characters onto a glass plate, perfume them with mastic and wash them with pure water and bury them beneath the door of your enemy and he will flee from you.*

*The Moon as above.*

*[190]*

## COMMENTARY:

The Latin in the title is the first half of verse two, *"O God my God, look upon me: why hast thou forsaken me?"* Ja Het is probably a corruption of Yah Heh, with the divine name Yah (meaning *'God'*, the divine name of the Sephira of Chokmah on the Tree of Life) with Heh, the Hebrew letter particularly associated with the soul and the Shekinah (divine feminine).

This Psalm is used in *Sepher Shimmush Tehillim* for protection when travelling. When travelling by sea it gives protection against pirates and storms, and when travelling by land, protection from men and beasts. The Psalm is prayed Psalm seven times daily with its divine name Aha (AH, the first half of AHIH, meaning *'I am'*, the divine name of the Qabalistic Sephira of Kether) along with the appropriate prayer.[87]

This Psalm is the second in the sequence of eight Psalms (8, 21, 27, 29, 32, 51, 72, 134) to be recited during the consecration of the Pentacles in the *Key of Solomon*. The Pentacle is held over the incense towards the rising sun and the Psalms recited with devotion.[88]

Verse fifteen, *"My heart is become like wax melting in the midst of my bowels"*, is written around the edge of a Venusian Pentacle which is used for exciting love (see Venus 5, Appendix 4).

Verses seventeen and eighteen *"They have dug my hands and feet. They have numbered all my bones"* is written around the edge of a Jupiterian Pentacle used for protection against earthly dangers (see Jupiter 6, Appendix 4).

Verse nineteen, *"They parted my garments amongst them; and upon my vesture they cast lots"* was appropriately used around the edge of a Mercurial Pentacle for games of chance (see Mercury 4, Appendix 5).

This Psalm is one of those in the sequence of nineteen (130, 14, 101, 8, 83, 67, 71, 132, 112, 125, 45, 46, 21, 50, 129, 138, 48, 109, 52) recited for conjuration of the wax used in making the Pentacles in the *Key of Solomon*.[89]

In the *Goetia* the second Shemhamphorash angel, Yeliel, is associated with verse twenty of this Psalm, *"But thou, O Lord, remove not thy help to a distance from me; look towards my defence"*.[90]

Verses twelve and twenty *"depart not from me. For tribulation is very near: for there is none to help me. But thou, O Lord, remove not thy help to a distance from me; look towards my defence"*, are combined in *A Treatise of Mixed Cabalah* to be delivered from all trials and tribulations.[91]

---

87 The Sixth and Seventh Books of Moses, Peterson, 2008:185.
88 The Veritable Key of Solomon, Skinner & Rankine, 2008:304.
89 The Key of Solomon the King, Mathers, 1976:114.
90 The Goetia of Dr Rudd, Skinner & Rankine, 2007:408.
91 A Collection of Magical Secrets, Skinner, Rankine & Barron,

In *Abramelin* a prayer based on verses ten and eleven is used for an easy birth. The prayer, *"I was birthed from the body of your mother, you are my god from the body of my mother, do not be distant from me, because fear is near and I have no helper except you alone, God Zebaoth"*, is written with olive oil on a silver spoon, fumigated, has the writing wiped off with the forefingers of the left hand and rubbed into the navel of the pregnant woman.[92]

---

2009:112.
92 The Book of Abramelin, Worms, Dehn & Guth, 2006:59.

# PSALM 22

## *Dominus regit me. Ah*

*If someone leaves with sorrow or leaves on any journey, let him read this Psalm and his enemies will not be able to withhold him and if he wanders from the path, let him read this Psalm over good oil and let him wash his face with it and he will find his path again. The Moon as above, hour of ☿.*

## COMMENTARY:

The Latin in the title is part of verse one, *"The Lord ruleth me"*. Ah is the first half of the divine name Eheieh (AH-IH, meaning *'I am'*, the divine name of the Sephira of Kether on the Tree of Life).

*Sepher Shimmush Tehillim* recommends this Psalm for receiving reliable instructions through a vision or a dream. The querent prepares himself by reciting the Psalm seven times with the appropriate prayer and the divine name Yah (IH, *'Lord'*) whilst fasting and bathing.[93]

This Psalm is one of those used in order to attain high honours, high rank and increase good fortune in the *Sepher Shimmush Tehillim*. The sequence is 91, 93, 22, 19, 23, 99 (see Psalm 91 for more details).[94]

Recited seven times with its associated names it was

---

93 The Sixth and Seventh Books of Moses, Peterson, 2008:185.
94 Ibid, Peterson, 2008:185.

said to give dream replies to questions.[95]

Verses three and four with *'The lord my shepherd'* added to the front, *"The lord my shepherd hath converted my soul. He hath led me on the paths of justice, for his own name's sake. For though I should walk in the midst of the shadow of death, I will fear no evils, for thou art with me. Thy rod and thy staff, they have comforted me"*, is given in *A Treatise of Mixed Cabalah* for being secure when passing through dubious and dangerous places.[96]

Verses five and six, *"Thou hast prepared a table before me against them that afflict me. Thou hast anointed my head with oil; and my chalice which inebriateth me, how goodly is it! And thy mercy will follow me all the days of my life. And that I may dwell in the house of the Lord unto length of days"*, is given in the same work for being provided with food and lodgings.[97]

95 Jewish Magic and Superstition, Trachtenberg, 1939:241.
96 A Collection of Magical Secrets, Skinner, Rankine & Barron, 2009:113.
97 Ibid, 2009:113.

# PSALM 23

## *Domini est terra & plenitude ejus. Jas*

*If someone wishes to be loved and to appear graceful, let him write this Psalm until* **Et introibit Rex Gloriæ** *along with the characters; perfume everything with musk, saffron and rose water and let him carry it upon himself.*

*The Moon as above, hour of* 4.

---

## COMMENTARY:

The Latin in the title is part of verse one, *"The earth is the Lord's and the fullness thereof"*.

*Sepher Shimmush Tehillim* gives this Psalm as being used for escaping great danger and avoiding floods, by repeating daily in the morning and using the holy name Eli (ALI, a poetic form of AL meaning *'God'*).[98]

This Psalm is one of those used in order to attain high honours, high rank and increase good fortune in the *Sepher Shimmush Tehillim*. The sequence is 91, 93, 22, 19, 23, 99 (see Psalm 91 for more details).[99]

Verse seven, *"Lift up your gates, O ye princes, and be ye lifted up, O eternal gates: and the King of Glory shall enter in"*

---

98 The Sixth and Seventh Books of Moses, Peterson, 2008:186.
99 Ibid, Peterson, 2008:186.

is used around the edge of a Mercurial Pentacle used for commanding Mercurial spirits and opening doors (see Mercury 5, Appendix 4).  It is also used on a Mercurial Pentacle against slavery and prison (see Mercury 2, Appendix 5).

# PSALM 24

## *Ad te Domine levavi animam meam*

*If a sick person cannot sleep, place this Psalm under his head and he will fall asleep. The Moon as above.*

## COMMENTARY:

The Latin in the title is the second half of verse one, *"To thee, O Lord, have I lifted up my soul"*.

As with the previous Psalm, *Sepher Shimmush Tehillim* gives this Psalm as being used for escaping great danger and avoiding floods, by repeating daily in the morning and using the holy name Eli (ALI, *'God'*).[100]

In the *Goetia*, the ninth Shemhamphorash angel, Aziel, is associated with verse six of this Psalm, *"Remember, O Lord, thy bowels of compassion; and thy mercies that are from the beginning of the world"*.[101]

Verses thirteen and fifteen, *"His soul shall dwell in good things: and his seed shall inherit the land. My eyes are ever towards the Lord: for he shall pluck my feet out of the snare"*, are used to make a sick man rest in *A Treatise of Mixed Cabalah*.[102]

---

100 The Sixth and Seventh Books of Moses, Peterson, 2008:186.
101 The Goetia of Dr Rudd, Skinner & Rankine, 2007:408.
102 A Collection of Magical Secrets, Skinner, Rankine & Barron, 2009:113.

# PSALM 25

## *Judica me Domine. El*

*If you want to destroy the workings of enchantments and fancies, it is necessary to write this Psalm and the enchanter will not be able to do anything against you and if you recite it in the midst of your enemies, you will be protected from them.*
*The Moon as above.*

*[191]*

## COMMENTARY:

The Latin in the title is part of verse one, *"Judge me, O Lord"*. El, meaning *'God'*, is the divine name of the Sephira of Chesed on the Qabalistic Tree of Life.

Again there is a degree of similarity in *Sepher Shimmush Tehillim,* where this Psalm is given with an appropriate prayer and the divine name Elohe (ALHI, *'God'*) for use against imminent dangers by land or by sea, or for someone about to receive a severe imprisonment.[103]

*A Treatise of Mixed Cabalah* gives a similar use with verses eleven and twelve, *"But as for me, I have walked in my innocence: redeem me, and have mercy on me. My foot hath stood in the direct way: in the churches I will bless thee, O Lord"*, to be spoken for delivery amidst enemies.[104]

---

103 The Sixth and Seventh Books of Moses, Peterson, 2008:186.
104 A Collection of Magical Secrets, Skinner, Rankine & Barron,

In the *Goetia*, the thirty-sixth Shemhamphorash angel, Menadel, is associated with verse eight of this Psalm, *"I have loved, O Lord, the beauty of thy house; and the place where thy glory dwelleth"*.[105]

2009:119.
105 The Goetia of Dr Rudd, Skinner & Rankine, 2007:410.

# PSALM 26

## *Dominus illumination mea & salus mea: Eloy.*

*If you wish to plant a vine tree, write this Psalm at the New Moon and wash it in a spring, which you will use to water your vine tree and it will be protected from all that is invisible. For children suffering with worms, write the 2ⁿᵈ and the 3ʳᵈ verses until* **Qui tribulant me inimici mei** *with three Pater's[106] and three Ave's[107] in the honour of the Saint whose name it bears.*

## COMMENTARY:

The Latin in the title is part of verse one, *"The Lord is my light and my salvation"*. Eloy is a divine name used in many of the grimoires, from *Liber Juratus* and the *Heptameron* through to the *Key of Solomon* and the *Goetia*.

*Sepher Shimmush Tehillim* states this Psalm is good for being well and kindly received in a strange city, and should be repeated while on your journey.[108]

---

106 "Our Father's".
107 "Hail Mary's".
108 The Sixth and Seventh Books of Moses, Peterson, 2008:186.

# PSALM 27

## *Ad te Domine clamabo. Selam.*

*It is good to those who confess that they suffer for their sins and by means of this, they can obtain all that they need from God, if they say it every day with devotion, as St Hierome[109] says. It is also good for those who are persecuted by their children and their close ones and as St Cassiodorus says, it is good for those who give alms, so that their possessions may be multiplied in this world and in the other.[110]*

*It reconciles us to our enemies and for this to take effect it is necessary to say it 3 times with the name of the Intelligence, while staring at his enemy opposite him, bending the middle finger onto the first phalanx of the index finger and to form the character with it. If you do this two times, you will have peace with him*

*[192]*

## COMMENTARY:

The Latin in the title is part of verse one, *"Unto thee will I cry, O Lord"*. The word Salem in the heading may be the intelligence name which is implied but not given in the text, particularly as it is derivative of the Arabic *salam* meaning

---

109 A variant spelling of St Jerome.
110 I.e. heaven.

*'peace'.*

Again one of the uses can be seen as being derived from *Sepher Shimmush Tehillim,* which gives this Psalm for reconciliation between you and your enemy, by reciting the Psalm with the divine name, He (HI, reversal of Yah) and an appropriate prayer.[111]

This Psalm is the third in the sequence of eight Psalms (8, 21, 27, 29, 32, 51, 72, 134) to be recited during the consecration of the Pentacles in the *Key of Solomon.* The Pentacle is held over the incense towards the rising sun and the Psalms recited with devotion.[112]

---

111 The Sixth and Seventh Books of Moses, Peterson, 2008:186.
112 The Veritable Key of Solomon, Skinner & Rankine, 2008:304.

# PSALM 28

## *Adferte Domino filii Dei: Ha Hay.*

*Should you recite this Psalm into the ear of a sick man, while he is taking barley beer, he will recover. Also write the Psalm down and bury it in the corners of a house with its characters and perfumed with nutmeg and you will enjoy great blessings from it.*

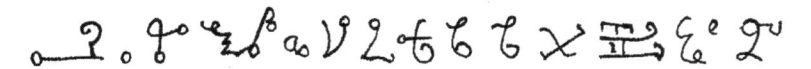

*The Moon as above.*

## COMMENTARY:

The Latin in the title is part of verse one, *"Bring to the Lord, O ye children of God"*.

There is an interesting procedure in *Sepher Shimmush Tehillim* using this Psalm to cast out evil spirits. Seven splinters of osier[113] and seven leaves of a date palm that never fruited are placed in a pot filled with water on which the sun has never shone. The Psalm is repeated over the pot ten times with the divine name Aha (AH) in the evening and left upon the earth in the open air until the next evening. The pot is then emptied at the door of the possessed person to drive the evil spirit out.[114]

Verses three to ten, containing seven references to the

---

113 A member of the willow family.
114 The Sixth and Seventh Books of Moses, Peterson, 2008:186.

'voice of God', were used as a protection when drinking water on nights when demons were particularly active, the implication being that they might enter the person in the water.[115] This probably derives from the practice of using water to contain demons, seen in the first century CE writings of Flavius Josephus.

This Psalm is recited in the process of detecting a thief using the Princes of the Cup with a sesame-oil anointed cup and two young virgin boys as seers in the eighteenth century text *Codex Gaster 214.*[116]

115 Jewish Magic and Superstition, Trachtenberg, 1939:109.
116 Babylonian Oil Magic, Daiches, 1913:25.

# PSALM 29

*Exaltabo te Domine quoniam suscepisti me: Ha*

*If someone languishes from a sickness, let him read this Psalm over pure water seven times and let him wash himself with the water and also read it 7 times over good oil, write the characters also and wash them with the aforementioned oil and anoint the sick man with it.*

*The Moon as above.*

---

## COMMENTARY:

The Latin in the title is the first half of verse two, *"I will extol thee, O Lord, for thou hast upheld me"*.

A similar use is given in *A Treatise of Mixed Cabalah*, where verses three and four, *"O Lord my God, I have cried to thee, and then hast healed me. Thou hast brought forth, O Lord, my soul from hell: thou hast saved me from them that go down into the pit"*, are used against a malevolent fever.[117]

According to *Sepher Shimmush Tehillim* this Psalm should be prayed daily with the divine name El (AL, *'God'*, the divine name of the Sephira of Chesed on the Qabalistic Tree of Life) for safety against all evil occurrences.[118]

This Psalm is the fourth in the sequence of eight Psalms

---

117 A Collection of Magical Secrets, Skinner, Rankine & Barron, 2009:120.
118 The Sixth and Seventh Books of Moses, Peterson, 2008:187

(8, 21, 27, 29, 32, 51, 72, 134) to be recited during the consecration of the Pentacles in the *Key of Solomon*. The Pentacle is held over the incense towards the rising sun and the Psalms recited with devotion.[119]

In the *Goetia*, the thirty-ninth Shemhamphorash angel, Rehael, is associated with verse eleven of this Psalm, *"The Lord hath heard, and hath had mercy on me: the Lord became my helper"*.[120]

---

119 The Veritable Key of Solomon, Skinner & Rankine, 2008:304.
120 The Goetia of Dr Rudd, Skinner & Rankine, 2007:410.

# PSALM 30

***In te Domine speravi, non confundar in æternum:***
***El.***

*If someone is held in a prison, let him read this Psalm until **Miserere mei Domine, quoniam triblor** two times a day and also at night, and let him also write these characters on bread and let him eat it; he will be freed from prison immediately.*

*The Moon as above.*
*[193]*

## COMMENTARY:

The Latin in the title is the first part of verse two, *"In thee, O Lord, have I hoped, let me never be confounded"*. El, meaning *'God'*, is the divine name of the Sephira of Chesed on the Qabalistic Tree of Life.

In *Sepher Shimmush Tehillim* this Psalm is repeated in a low voice over olive oil which is used to anoint the face and hands whilst concentrating on the divine name Yah (IH, *'God'*) to escape harm from slander and evil tongues.[121]

Verse two of this Psalm, *"In thee, O Lord, have I hoped, let me never be confounded: deliver me in thy justice"*, is given for writing on a chimney with fired charcoal and the words

---

121 The Sixth and Seventh Books of Moses, Peterson, 2008:187.

'Tetragrammaton, consummatum est.'[122] (*John 19:30*) for extinguishing fire in the *Key of Solomon.*[123]

This is the third Psalm in the sequence of seven (3, 8, 30, 41, 59, 50, 129) for use in the preparation of the needle, burin and other iron instruments in the *Key of Solomon.*[124]

In the *Goetia*, the twenty-first Shemhamphorash angel, Nelakael, is associated with verse fifteen of this Psalm, *"But I have put my trust in thee, O Lord: I said: Thou art my God"*.[125]

---

122 "Tetragrammaton, it is done".
123 The Veritable Key of Solomon, Skinner & Rankine, 2008:259.
124 The Key of Solomon the King, Mathers, 1976:115.
125 The Goetia of Dr Rudd, Skinner & Rankine, 2007:409.

# PSALM 31

## *Beati quorum remissæ sunt iniquitates:*

*If someone is tempted by the spirit of fornication, let him read this Psalm over holy water at the Epiphany of the Lord 7 times, let him wash himself with it and let him write these characters, perfume them with mastic and let him tie them to his arm and his desires will be extinguished.*

*The Moon as above.*

## COMMENTARY:

The Latin in the title is part of verse one, *"Blessed are they whose iniquities are forgiven"*.

This Psalm is one of the seven Penitential Psalms.

This Psalm should be recited daily to receive grace, love and mercy according to *Sepher Shimmush Tehillim*.[126]

Verse nine, *"Do not become like the horse and the mule, who have no understanding. With bit and bridle bind fast their jaws, who come not near unto thee"*, is given to prevent being bitten by any dog or serpent in *A Treatise of Mixed Cabalah*.[127]

---

126 The Sixth and Seventh Books of Moses, Peterson, 2008:188.
127 A Collection of Magical Secrets, Skinner, Rankine & Barron, 2009:114.

# PSALM 32

*Exultate Justi in Domino: Adonay.*

*Against a woman's sterility; write this Psalm along with the characters and perfume them with mastic and incense and attach them to the right arm of the woman and when she lies with her husband, she will conceive.*

*The Moon in ♍ or in ♌ hour of ♃.*

## COMMENTARY:

The Latin in the title is part of verse one, *"Rejoice in the Lord, O ye just"*. Adonay (ADNI), meaning *'Lord'* is the divine name substituted for Tetragrammaton (IHVH) in Judaism, which has become one of the main divine names in the grimoires and the Qabalah.

Once again the derivation from *Sepher Shimmush Tehillim* is clear, as that text recommends reciting this Psalm with the divine name Jahveh (IHVH, the Tetragrammaton) over pure olive oil and anointing a woman with it if she suffers with stillborn children. It is also declared to be good during times of famine.[128]

This Psalm is the fifth in the sequence of eight Psalms (8, 21, 27, 29, 32, 51, 72, 134) to be recited during the consecration of the Pentacles in the *Key of Solomon*. The Pentacle is held over the incense towards the rising sun and the Psalms recited with devotion.[129]

In the *Goetia*, three of the Shemhamphorash angels are associated with verses of this Psalm. These are the tenth angel, Aladiah with verse twenty-two, *"Let thy mercy, O Lord, be upon us, as we have hoped in thee"*;[130] the thirty-second, angel Vashariah with verse four, *"For the word of the Lord is right, and all his works are done with faithfulness"*;[131] and the sixty-fourth angel, Mechiel, with verse eighteen, *"Behold the eyes of the Lord are on them that fear him: and on them that hope in his mercy"*.[132]

---

128 The Sixth and Seventh Books of Moses, Peterson, 2008:188.
129 Veritable Key of Solomon, Skinner & Rankine, 2008:304.
130 The Goetia of Dr Rudd, Skinner & Rankine, 2007:408.
131 Ibid, 2007:410.
132 Ibid, 2007:412.

# PSALM 33

*Benedicam Dominum in omni tempore.*

*If someone has toothache or has a fractured bone, let him take some date stones[133] to a crossroad and let him read out the above Psalm 7 times until **Unum ex his non conteretur** and let him perfume his face with smoke and he will be healed.*
*The Moon and hour as above.*
*[194]*

## COMMENTARY:

The Latin in the title is the first half of verse two, *"I will bless the Lord at all times"*.

The implication is that the date stones are burned to create the smoke for perfuming the face.

The same purpose of healing toothache or bone fracture is seen in *A Treatise of Mixed Cabalah*, with verses thirteen and twenty-one, *"Who is the man that desireth life: who loveth to see good days? The Lord keepeth all their bones, not one of them shall be broken"*, given for recitation.[134]

The third century CE Christian historian Sextus Julius Africanus prescribed writing the first half of Verse 9, *"O taste, and see that the Lord is sweet"* on an apple and thrown

---

133 I.e. Phoenix dactylifera.
134 A Collection of Magical Secrets, Skinner, Rankine & Barron, 2009:120.

into a wine cask to stop it going sour.[135]

In the eleventh century Hekhalot text *Tefillat Hamnuna Sava (The Prayer by Hamnuna the Elder)*, this Psalm is repeated thrice by the mystic in his preparation, as part of the instructions given by the archangel Sagnasgiel (Metatron). This is followed by a triple recitation of the Ashre prayer, which is centred on Psalm 144.[136]

In *Sepher Shimmush Tehillim* this Psalm is recommended to be recited with the divine name Pele (PLA, *'Wonderful'*) before appearing in front of a prince or person in high authority to be well received.[137]

In the *Goetia*, the fifth Shemhamphorash angel Mahasiah is associated with verse five of this Psalm, *"I sought the Lord, and he heard me; and he delivered me from all my troubles"*.[138]

135 Art, Medicine and Magic in Early Byzantium, Vikan, 1984:70.
136 Jewish Mysticism in the Geonic Period, Herrmann, 2005:184
137 The Sixth and Seventh Books of Moses, Peterson, 2008:188.
138 The Goetia of Dr Rudd, Skinner & Rankine, 2007:408.

# PSALM 34

***Judica Domine nocentes me.***

*If you fall into need, recite this Psalm 7 times and you will come out of it and if you wish to have access to a Prince or to your enemies, write this Psalm and attach it to your arm and God will deliver you. The Moon and hour as before.*

## ORATION

*Oh God Almighty and Saviour of our fleeting infatuations, guard us from them through your Holy Spirit and protect us with Thy invisible shield, so that the aid that Thou grantest us in our need and necessity will make us worthy to enjoy the same joy and the same satisfaction as those whom Thou blessest in Heaven through our Lord Jesus Christ. So Mote it be.*

## COMMENTARY:

The Latin in the title is part of verse one, *"Judge thou, O Lord, them that wrong me"*.

There is a degree of similarity here with *Sepher Shimmush Tehillim,* which recommends praying this Psalm with the divine name Yah (IH, *'God'*) early in the morning for three successive days to win lawsuits instigated by unlawful, unrighteous, revengeful or quarrelsome people.[139]

In the *Goetia*, the eighteenth Shemhamphorash angel Kaliel, is associated with verse twenty-four of this Psalm, *"Judge me, O Lord my God according to thy justice, and let them not rejoice over me"*.[140]

Verses five and six, *"Let them become as dust before the wind: and let the angel of the Lord straighten them. Let their way become dark and slippery; and let the angel of the Lord pursue them"*, are given for protection from persecution by powerful men and tyrants in *A Treatise of Mixed Cabalah*.[141]

139 The Sixth and Seventh Books of Moses, Peterson, 2008:188.
140 The Goetia of Dr Rudd, Skinner & Rankine, 2007:409.
141 A Collection of Magical Secrets, Skinner, Rankine & Barron, 2009:115.

# PSALM 35

## *Dixit injustus ut delinquatim semet ipso: Ja*

*If a woman is pregnant, write this Psalm and fix it onto the hood of the robe that she is wearing or tie it to the right arm under her robe and her fruit will be preserved securely until its birth.*
*The Moon as above.*

## COMMENTARY:

The Latin in the title is the first half of verse two, *"The unjust hath said within himself, that he would sin"*. Ja occurs in the *Heptameron* as a divine name, and may be a contraction of Yah.

A similar use is seen in *A Treatise of Mixed Cabalah* where a version of verse eight with verse ten, *"O how hast thou multiplied thy mercy, O God! But the children of men shall put their trust under the covert of thy wings. For with thee is the fountain of life; and in thy light we shall see light"*, is given for making a woman give birth without pain.[142]

*Sepher Shimmush Tehillim* recommends this Psalm for use against all evil and slanderous libels. The Psalm is recited with the divine name Amet (AMTh, *'Truth'*).[143]

---

142 A Collection of Magical Secrets, Skinner, Rankine & Barron, 2009:114.
143 The Sixth and Seventh Books of Moses, Peterson, 2008:188.

# PSALM 36

## *Noli Æmulari in malignantibus: Eh*

*Write this Psalm and bury it in front of the door of your enemy. His house will be destroyed, his children will die and [195] all that he possesses will perish.*
*The Moon as above.*

## COMMENTARY:

The Latin in the title is part of verse one, *"Be not emulous of evildoers"*. Eh could be a variant of Ah, the first half of the divine name Eheieh (*'I am'*).

A drunkenness cure is given in *Sepher Shimmush Tehillim* for those who have drunk too much wine, lost their reason and may be fearful for their safety. Water is poured into a pitcher and the Psalm recited over it, and the head and face bathed in the water, with some of it being drunk.[144]

Verse 15, *"Let their sword enter into their own hearts, and let their bow be broken"* is used in a Martial Pentacle which is used for protection when fighting, with the weapons of enemies being turned against them (see Mars 6, Appendix 4). There are also two derivative Martial Pentacles from this, for being invulnerable and charming weapons, and to encourage civil wars in foreign countries (see Mars 5 & Mars 8, Appendix 5).

In the *Goetia*, the sixty-seventh Shemhamphorash angel,

---

144 The Sixth and Seventh Books of Moses, Peterson, 2008:188.

Eiael, is associated with verse four of this Psalm, *"Delight in the Lord, and he will give thee the requests of thy heart"*.[145]

In *A Treatise of Mixed Cabalah*, verses thirty-nine and forty, *"And the Lord will help them and deliver them: and he will rescue them from the wicked, and save them, because they have hoped in him"*, is given to confound an armed enemy so he will not harm you.[146]

---

145 The Goetia of Dr Rudd, Skinner & Rankine, 2007:415.
146 A Collection of Magical Secrets, Skinner, Rankine & Barron, 2009:114.

# PSALM 37

*Domine ne in furore tuo arguas me, Eye.*

*If someone has pain in his eyes, let him read out this Psalm over holy water at Christmas, let him wash his eyes with it and let him write these characters also and let him perfume them with mastic and with incense and let him hang them from his neck.*

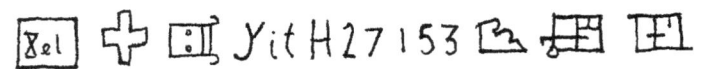

## COMMENTARY:

The Latin in the title is the first half of verse two, *"Rebuke me not, O Lord, in thy indignation"*. Eye is a name found in conjurations in various grimoires including the *Heptameron*, *Key of Solomon* and *Goetia*.

This is the third of the seven Penitential Psalms.

This Psalm is recommended by *Sepher Shimmush Tehillim* for those fearing punishment from the king and officers of the law due to slander. The Psalm should be recited at daybreak in a field with the divine name Aha (AH) seven times, and the person should fast the entire day.[147]

A similar use against blindness is seen in *A Treatise of Mixed Cabalah*, with recitation of verse eleven, *"My heart is troubled, my strength hath left me, and the light of my eyes itself is not with me"*.[148] The same text also gives verses four

---

147 The Sixth and Seventh Books of Moses, Peterson, 2008:188.
148 A Collection of Magical Secrets, Skinner, Rankine & Barron,

and five, *"here is no health in my flesh, because of thy wrath: there is no peace for my bones, because of my sins. For my iniquities are gone over my head: and as a heavy burden are become heavy upon me"*, as a charm against muteness.[149]

In the *Goetia*, the sixty-sixth Shemhamphorash angel, Manaqel, is associated with verse twenty-two, *"Forsake me not, O Lord my God: do not thou depart from me"*.[150]

2009:121.
149 Ibid, 2009:121.
150 The Goetia of Dr Rudd, Skinner & Rankine, 2007:415.

# PSALM 38

## *Dixi custodiam vias meas. Day*

*If you are tormented by bad dreams, write this Psalm on the right side of your face but do not speak at all and you will have no more bad dreams.*
*The Moon as above this one.*

## COMMENTARY:

The Latin in the title is the beginning of verse two, *"I said: I will take heed to my ways"*.

This Psalm is recommended by *Sepher Shimmush Tehillim* for those fearing punishment from the king and officers of the law due to slander. The Psalm should be recited at daybreak in a field with the divine name He (HI) seven times, and the person should fast the entire day.[151]

---

151 The Sixth and Seventh Books of Moses, Peterson, 2008:188.

# PSALM 39

*Expectans expectavi Dominum*

*If a woman cannot hold in her fruit,[152] write this Psalm*
*with the characters and tie them to her right arm and*
*she will hold on to it.*

*⟨magical characters⟩*

## COMMENTARY:

The Latin in the title is the first half of verse two, *"With expectation I have waited for the Lord"*.

*Sepher Shimmush Tehillim* states that when this Psalm is prayed daily with the divine name Yah (IH, *'God'*) it frees people from evil spirits.[153]

Verse 14, *"Be pleased, O Lord, to deliver me, look down, O Lord, to help me"* is written around the edge of a Lunar Pentacle which is used for protection against attacks at night and all kinds of danger associated with water (see Moon 3, Appendix 4).

In the *Goetia*, the nineteenth Shemhamphorash angel, Leuviah, is associated with verse two of this Psalm, *"With expectation I have waited for the Lord, and he was attentive to me"*.[154]

---

152 Is at risk of miscarrying.
153 The Sixth and Seventh Books of Moses, Peterson, 2008:189.
154 The Goetia of Dr Rudd, Skinner & King, 2007:412.

# PSALM 40

## *Beatus qui intelligit super egenum & pauperem:*

*If you have a woman or a mistress whom you hate or you [196] mistrust, read this Psalm 7 times over rose oil, anoint your face with it and you will overcome her and write these characters on the parchment skin of a young billy-goat, perfume them with some of the oil, with saffron and with rose water; write the name of the woman on it also and take some of her hair and anoint them with it and bury it all in front of her door.*

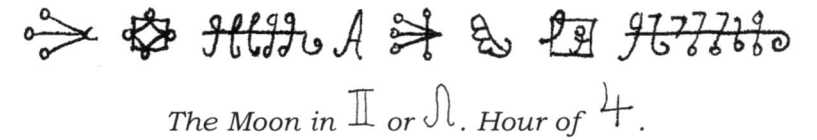

*The Moon in* ♊ *or* ♌. *Hour of* ♃.

## COMMENTARY:

The Latin in the title is the first half of verse two, *"Blessed is he that understandeth concerning the needy and the poor".*

*Sepher Shimmush Tehillim* advises praying Psalms 40 to 42 three times a day for three successive days for protection against ruined credit and mistrust of others causing reduction in earnings or loss of office caused by enemies.[155]

In *A Treatise of Mixed Cabalah*, verse three, *"The Lord preserve him and give him life, and make him blessed upon the earth: and deliver him not up to the will of his enemies"*, is

---

155 The Sixth and Seventh Books of Moses, Peterson, 2008:189.

described as being used to be raised up with dignity by everyone. [156]

The same work gives verses four and five, *"The Lord help him on his bed of sorrow: thou hast turned all his couch in his sickness. I said: O Lord, be thou merciful to me: heal my soul, for I have sinned against thee"*, for use against fever. [157]

156 A Collection of Magical Secrets, Skinner, Rankine & Barron, 2009:110.
157 Ibid, 2009:121.

# PSALM 41

## Quem admodum desiderat cervus ad fontes aquarum

*Recite this Psalm three times at the hour of Vespers[158] and your enemies will be dispersed and they will have no power over you.*

## COMMENTARY:

The Latin in the title is the first half of verse two, *"As the hart panteth after the fountains of water"*.

*Sepher Shimmush Tehillim* advises praying Psalms 40 to 42 three times a day for three successive days for protection against ruined credit and mistrust of others causing reduction in earnings or loss of office caused by enemies.[159]

This is the fourth Psalm in the sequence of seven (3, 8, 30, 41, 59, 50, 129) for use in the preparation of the needle, burin and other iron instruments in the *Key of Solomon*.[160]

An adapted version of verse two is used in *Munich CLM 849* in an experiment to gain the passionate love of a woman, *"as the hart longs for the fountain of water, so you, N., should long for my love"*.[161] Recited seven times with its associated names it was said to give dream replies to questions.[162]

---

158 The evening prayer service.
159 The Sixth and Seventh Books of Moses, Peterson, 2008:189.
160 The Key of Solomon the King, Mathers, 1976:115.
161 Forbidden Rites, Kieckhefer, 1997:142.
162 Jewish Magic and Superstition, Trachtenberg, 1939:241.

# PSALM 42

*Judica me Deus & discerne causam meam de gente. Jahu*

*If someone wishes to have access to a King or to a Prince, let him write this Psalm and attach it to his right arm and he will be honourably received. The Moon as above.*

## COMMENTARY:

The Latin in the title is part of verse one, *"Judge me, O God, and distinguish my cause from the nation that is not holy"*. Jahu is a divine name made of the first three letters of Tetragrammaton, Yod Heh Vav (IHV).

The fourteenth century *De Sigillis* of pseudo-Arnaldus used this Psalm, to be recited whilst preparing the talisman of Leo for protection of the kidneys, and stomach, and from abscesses and fevers.[163]

*Sepher Shimmush Tehillim* advises praying Psalms 40 to 42 three times a day for three successive days for protection against ruined credit and mistrust of others causing reduction in earnings or loss of office caused by enemies.[164]

The same text also advises using this Psalm if you wish to receive information through dreaming. The person should fast for a day and then pray this Psalm seven times with the divine name Tzava (TzBA, *'Hosts'*, as in Lord of Hosts)

---

163 Binding Words, Skemer, 2006:132.
164 The Sixth and Seventh Books of Moses, Peterson, 2008:189.

naming your wishes before retiring to bed.[165]

In *Munich CLM 849* this Psalm is one of two used (with Psalm 50) for the purpose of obtaining a flying throne.[166]

165 Ibid, Peterson, 2008:189.
166 Forbidden Rites, Kieckhefer, 1997:232.

# PSALM 43

## *Deus auribus nostris audivimus*

*Write this Psalm with bird's blood and bury it in front of the door of your enemy and he will be destroyed. The Moon as above.*

## COMMENTARY:

The Latin in the title is the beginning of verse two, *"We have heard, O God, with our ears"*.

According to *Sepher Shimmush Tehillim* this Psalm should be prayed frequently to be safe from enemies.[167] From here the use has become more proactive with action to destroy the enemy.

---

167 The Sixth and Seventh Books of Moses, Peterson, 2008:189.

# PSALM 44

## *Eructavit cor meum verbum bonum*

*Write this Psalm and the name of the one you desire, at the waxing of the [197] Moon until **Quoniam ipse est Dominus Deus tuus & adoreabunt eum** and perfume them with myrrh, aromatic gum and cinnamon and bury it in front of her door and you will be loved by her; it is also good against those who seek to ensnare you under the pretext of offering favours.*

*The moon in ♊ or ♍. Hour of ♃.*

## COMMENTARY:

The Latin in the title is the beginning of verse one, *"My heart hath uttered a good word"*.

Again the use seems to have been derived and adapted from *Sepher Shimmush Tehillim,* which advises husbands to recite this Psalm over olive oil and anoint their body to make a scolding wife more lovable and friendly in future, with the divine name Adoya (ADIH, being a composite of Adonai and Jahveh).[168]

---

168 The Sixth and Seventh Books of Moses, Peterson, 2008:189.

# PSALM 45

## *Deus noster refugium & virtus: Arie*

*If you need to enter into armed combat, read this Psalm until **et scuta cumburet in igni** seven times and no one will withstand against you.*

## COMMENTARY:

The Latin in the title is the beginning of verse two, *"Our God is our refuge and strength"*.

For this Psalm, *Sepher Shimmush Tehillim* declares that when a husband has innocently angered his wife, he should pray the Psalm over olive oil and anoint his wife with it, whilst thinking of the divine name Adoya (ADIH).[169]

Psalm is one of those in the sequence of nineteen (130, 14, 101, 8, 83, 67, 71, 132, 112, 125, 45, 46, 21, 50, 129, 138, 48, 109, 52) recited for conjuration of the wax used in making the Pentacles in the *Key of Solomon*.[170]

---

169 The Sixth and Seventh Books of Moses, Peterson, 2008:189.
170 The Key of Solomon the King, Mathers, 1976:114.

# PSALM 46

## *Omnes gentes plaudite manibus; Sale*

*If you wish to be lucky in all manner of affairs, you write the Psalm and carry it on you and read it 7 times a day and that, which you desire will come to you in all goodness and your enemies will not be able to harm you. The Moon as above.*

## COMMENTARY:

The Latin in the title is the first half of verse two, *"O clap your hands, all ye nations"*.

This use, *'To be lucky in all things'*, is also seen in *The Keys of Rabbi Solomon*, one of the three main families of *Key of Solomon* manuscripts. The person is instructed to say the Psalm before sunrise and before eating.[171]

As with many of the other uses in *Le Livre d'Or*, the precedent from *Sepher Shimmush Tehillim* suggests its origins. According to the latter work, this Psalm should be prayed seven times daily to be loved and well-received by all your fellow men.[172]

Psalm 46 is the fourth of the sequence of five Psalms (2, 53, 50, 46, 67) given in the *Key of Solomon* to be recited before or during the creation of the magic circle.[173]

This Psalm is one of those in the sequence of nineteen

---

171 The Veritable Key of Solomon, Skinner & Rankine, 2008:259.
172 The Sixth and Seventh Books of Moses, Peterson, 2008:189.
173 Ibid, 2008:286.

(130, 14, 101, 8, 83, 67, 71, 132, 112, 125, 45, 46, 21, 50, 129, 138, 48, 109, 52) recited for conjuration of the wax used in making the Pentacles in the *Key of Solomon*.[174]

Verse four, *"He hath subdued the people under us; and the nations under our feet"* is used as part of a coercive binding spell to gain favour with a dignitary in *Munich CLM 849*.[175]

In *A Treatise of Mixed Cabalah*, verses three and four, *"For the Lord is high, terrible: a great king over all the earth. He hath subdued the people under us; and the nations under our feet"*, are given for being pleasing to all men and to obtain their favour. [176]

In the same work, verses three and five, *"For the Lord is high, terrible: a great king over all the earth. He hath chosen for us his inheritance the beauty of Jacob which he hath loved"*, is given to be lucky in all your affairs.[177]

---

174 The Key of Solomon the King, Mathers, 1976:114.
175 Forbidden Rites, Kieckhefer, 1997:77.
176 A Collection of Magical Secrets, Skinner, Rankine & Barron, 2009:111.
177 Ibid, 2009:114.

# PSALM 47

## *Magnus Dominus & landabilis nimis civitate dei: Saday*

*If there has been a theft in your house, write this Psalm with its characters and place it above your head in the bed and you will see the thief.*

*the Moon in* ♋ *or* ♓. *Hour of* ♃
[198]

## COMMENTARY:

The Latin in the title is most of verse two, *"Great is the Lord, and exceedingly to be praised in the city of our God"*. Saday is a spelling of the divine name Shaddai (ShDI, *'Almighty'*, a divine name of the Sephira of Yesod on the Qabalistic Tree of Life).

In the fourth century text *Corpus Hippiatricorum Graecorum* (10.3.5), advice is given to write verses two to seven on papyrus and place it on a mare having trouble giving birth as a remedy.[178]

According to *Sepher Shimmush Tehillim* this Psalm prayed often whilst thinking of the divine name Zach (ZCh, *'Pure, Clear & Transparent'*) will seize spiteful and envious

---

178 Magic in the Ancient Greek World, Collins, 2008:129.

enemies with fear, terror and anxiety so they bother you no more.[179]

This Psalm is spoken after fumigating oneself with frankincense and lignum aloes before entering the circle in *De Nigromancia* of Roger Bacon.[180]

A spell in order to find lost objects which includes this Psalm is found in *A Collection of Magical Secrets*.[181]

179 The Sixth and Seventh Books of Moses, Peterson, 2008:189.
180 De Nigromancia, Bacon, 1988:32.
181 A Collection of Magical Secrets, Skinner, Rankine & Barron, 2009:23.

# PSALM 48

*Audite hæc omnes gentes:*

*If you love someone and you wish to be honoured by her, write this Psalm until* **Verumtamen Deus remediet animam meam de manu inferi** *and carry it on you. You will be loved and cherished.*

## COMMENTARY:

The Latin in the title is the beginning of verse two, *"Hear these things, all ye nations"*.

*Sepher Shimmush Tehillim* recommends this Psalm for a family member sick with an incurable fever. With a new pen and ink write out the Psalm with the first six verses of Psalm 50, together with the appropriate divine name, Shaddai (ShDI, *'Almighty'*) on pure parchment, and hang it around the patient's neck with a silken string.[182]

This Psalm is one of those in the sequence of nineteen (130, 14, 101, 8, 83, 67, 71, 132, 112, 125, 45, 46, 21, 50, 129, 138, 48, 109, 52) recited for conjuration of the wax used in making the Pentacles in the *Key of Solomon*.[183]

This Psalm is the first of three written with some characters on a piece of virgin parchment and placed under the pillow for a dream vision of a thief and where he placed stolen goods.[184]

---

182 The Sixth and Seventh Books of Moses, Peterson, 2008:190.
183 The Key of Solomon the King, Mathers, 1976:114.
184 A Collection of Magical Secrets, Skinner, Rankine & Barron, 2009:23.

# PSALM 49

*Deus Deorum Dominus Locutus est: H Hay.*

*If you wish to kill a sheep and distribute it amongst the poor, read this Psalm seven times until* **Holocausta autem tua in conspectu meo sunt semper.** *God will love you.*

## COMMENTARY:

The Latin in the title is part of verse one, *"The God of gods, the Lord hath spoken"*.

*Sepher Shimmush Tehillim* recommends this Psalm as part of the cure for a family member sick with an incurable fever. With a new pen and ink write out Psalm 49 with the first six verses of this Psalm, together with the appropriate divine name, Shaddai (ShDI, *'Almighty'*) on pure parchment, and hang it around the patient's neck with a silken string. [185] The same text recommends wearing this Psalm in a similar manner to protect its wearer from all dangers and especially robbers, using instead the divine name Chi (ChI, *'Living'*). [186]

In the *Key of Solomon* this Psalm is used as part of the process of bibliomancy with the bible and a key called the *Operation of the Divinatory Key*. The Psalm is recited to the end of verse 21, and the resultant place marked by the key at this moment is the answer to the question posed by the querent.[187]

---

185 The Sixth and Seventh Books of Moses, Peterson, 2008:190.
186 Ibid, Peterson, 2008:190.
187 The Veritable Key of Solomon, Skinner & Rankine, 2008:254-5.

# PSALM 50

## *Miserere mei Deus: Ram.*

*Write this Psalm on a person who suffers from bleeding, either born with it[188] or otherwise, until **Deus salutis meæ***

*The Moon as above.*

## COMMENTARY:

The Latin in the title is the opening words of verse three, *"Have mercy on me, O God"*.

This is the fourth of the seven Penitential Psalms.

It is the first of the five Psalms in the sequence for preparing the holy drink against elf influence and the devil's temptations in the *Lacnunga* manuscript (C10th-11th CE).[189]

*Sepher Shimmush Tehillim* recommends this Psalm for those troubled by a heavy conscience on account of a grievous sin. The Psalm is recited three times with an appropriate prayer whilst contemplating the word Dam (DM, *'Blood'*), mentioning the evil deed. This is performed three times a day over poppy oil, which is used to anoint the body and remove the burden.[190]

Psalm 50 is the third of the sequence of five Psalms (2, 53, 50, 46, 67) given in the *Key of Solomon* to be recited

---

188 I.e. hæmophilia.
189 Leechcraft, Pollington, 2004:193.
190 The Sixth and Seventh Books of Moses, Peterson, 2008:190.

before or during the creation of the magic circle.[191]

Verse nine, *"Thou shalt sprinkle me with hyssop, and I shall be cleansed: thou shalt wash me, and I shall be made whiter than snow"* is used in the *Key of Solomon* for the exorcism of water.[192] This verse is also used in the preparation for the creation of a cloak of invisibility in *Munich CLM 849.*[193]

This Psalm up to verse 8 is also given as an alternative to be used for the *Operation of the Divinatory Key* in the *Key of Solomon.*[194]

This Psalm is one of those in the sequence of nineteen (130, 14, 101, 8, 83, 67, 71, 132, 112, 125, 45, 46, 21, 50, 129, 138, 48, 109, 52) recited for conjuration of the wax used in making the Pentacles in the *Key of Solomon.*[195]

This is the sixth Psalm in the sequence of seven (3, 8, 30, 41, 59, 50, 129) for use in the preparation of the needle, burin and other iron instruments in the *Key of Solomon.*[196]

In *Munich CLM 849* this Psalm is one of two used (with Psalm 42) for the purpose of obtaining a flying throne.[197] It is also spoken in full whilst gazing devotedly at a crucifix as part of the experiment to discover hidden treasure in the same text.[198] A further use in this text is in obtaining information from a mirror.[199]

In *A Treatise of Mixed Cabalah*, a technique is given for discovering a hidden object. This is done by taking a ring without a bezel or stone, tying a thread to it and suspending it in the middle of a glass of water and reciting verse eight, *"For behold thou hast loved truth: the uncertain and hidden*

---

191 The Veritable Key of Solomon, Skinner & Rankine, 2008:286.
192 Ibid, 2008:340.
193 Forbidden Rites, Kieckhefer, 1997:59.
194 The Veritable Key of Solomon, Skinner & Rankine, 2008:254.
195 The Key of Solomon the King, Mathers, 1976:114.
196 Ibid, 1976:115.
197 Forbidden Rites, Kieckhefer, 1997:232.
198 Ibid, 1997:77.
199 Ibid, 1997:287.

*things of thy wisdom thou hast made manifest to me"*.[200]

Verse sixteen of this Psalm, *"Deliver me from blood, O God, thou God of my salvation: and my tongue shall extol thy justice"*, is recommended in the same work against nose bleeds and haemorrhages in other parts of the body.[201]

---

200 A Collection of Magical Secrets, Skinner, Rankine & Barron, 2009:119.
201 Ibid, 2009:120.

# PSALM 51

## *Quid gloriaris in malitia. Ay.*

*If a pregnant woman corrupts[202] her fruit, write this Psalm and attach it to her arm and she will be healed. The Moon as above*

## COMMENTARY:

The Latin in the title is the first half of verse three, *"Why dost thou glory in malice"*. Ay is a name found in conjurations in *Liber Juratus* and the *Heptameron*.

This Psalm is recommended for daily morning prayer by *Sepher Shimmush Tehillim* for those victimised by slander.[203]

This Psalm is the sixth in the sequence of eight Psalms (8, 21, 27, 29, 32, 51, 72, 134) to be recited during the consecration of the Pentacles in the *Key of Solomon*. The Pentacle is held over the incense towards the rising sun and the Psalms recited with devotion.[204]

---

202 Possibly suffering with syphilis.
203 The Sixth and Seventh Books of Moses, Peterson, 2008:190.
204 The Veritable Key of Solomon, Skinner & Rankine, 2008:304.

# PSALM 52

*Dixit incipiens in corde suo*

*Take some powder in your hand and read this Psalm 7 times over it [199] with devotion and throw this dust into the face of your enemies; with the aid of God, they will flee immediately from before you.*

*The Moon in ♋ or in ♓ hour of the ☽.*

## COMMENTARY:

The Latin in the title is part of verse one, *"The fool said in his heart"*.

The roots of this use again may well be in *Sepher Shimmush Tehillim,* which recommends reciting this Psalm daily with the divine name Ai (AI, the first letters of Adonai and Jahveh) to quieten enemies or fill them with fear.[205]

This is the second of the sequence of three Psalms (60, 52, 56) to be spoken over the candles to purify them prior to consecration in the *Key of Solomon.*[206]

This Psalm is one of those in the sequence of nineteen (130, 14, 101, 8, 83, 67, 71, 132, 112, 125, 45, 46, 21, 50, 129, 138, 48, 109, 52) recited for conjuration of the wax used in making the Pentacles in the *Key of Solomon.*[207]

---

205 The Sixth and Seventh Books of Moses, Peterson, 2008:191.
206 The Key of Solomon the King, Mathers, 1976:104.
207 Ibid, 1976:114.

# PSALM 53

## Deus in nomine tuo salvum me fac: Va.

*If someone is slandered and brought before the Prince or some other Lord, let him read this Psalm 7 times in his supplication and he will be delivered.*

## COMMENTARY:

The Latin in the title is the first half of verse three, *"Save me, O God, by thy name"*. Va is a name found in conjurations in the *Heptameron*.

*Sepher Shimmush Tehillim* recommends this Psalm with the divine name Yah (IH) to avenge or protect oneself, suggesting the likely source of *Le Livre d'Or*'s attribution.[208]

It is the second of the five Psalms in the sequence for preparing the holy drink against elf influence and the devil's temptations in the *Lacnunga* manuscript (C10th-11th CE).[209]

This Psalm is used prior to skrying in the crystal by the virgin child in the fifteenth century *Sloane MS 3849*.[210]

Psalm 53 is the second of the sequence of five Psalms (2, 53, 50, 46, 67) given in the *Key of Solomon* to be recited before or during the creation of the magic circle.[211] It is also the last in the sequence of three Psalms (2, 66, 53) to be spoken on entering a room or outdoor space for a ceremony

---

208 The Sixth and Seventh Books of Moses, Peterson, 2008:191.
209 Leechcraft, Pollington, 2004:193.
210 Crystal Gazing, Thomas, 1905:83.
211 The Veritable Key of Solomon, Skinner & Rankine, 2009:286.

before taking any action.[212]

In the *Goetia*, the twenty-ninth Shemhamphorash angel, Reiyel, is associated with verse of this Psalm, *"For behold God is my helper: and the Lord is the protector of my soul"*.[213]

This Psalm written by a virgin child with part of the Pater Noster and touched to a newborn child was used to make a talisman for receiving goodwill and favours.[214]

212 Ibid, 2009:342.
213 The Goetia of Dr Rudd, Skinner & King, 2007:411.
214 A Collection of Magical Secrets, Skinner, Rankine & Barron, 2009:82.

# PSALM 54

### *Exaudi orationem meam & ne despexeris deprecationem.*

*If your enemy builds a house and you wish to prevent him from completing it, read this Psalm over the foundations; he will not be able to build it. The Moon as above.*

## COMMENTARY:

The Latin in the title is verse two, *"Hear, O God, my prayer, and despise not my supplication"*.

To return evil for evil, *Sepher Shimmush Tehillim* gives this Psalm with the divine name Vah (VH, the second half of Tetragrammaton).[215]

In the *Key of Solomon* this Psalm is one of the three spoken to prepare a room for use, so this is an interesting similarity, as here magic is being used to prevent a place being used.[216]

It is also the third Psalm in the sequence of five Psalms (17, 13, 54, 80, 117) to be recited whilst bathing before conjuration in the *Key of Solomon*.[217]

---

215 The Sixth and Seventh Books of Moses, Peterson, 2008:191.
216 The Veritable Key of Solomon, Skinner & Rankine, 2008:342.
217 Ibid, 2008:341.

# PSALM 55

*Miserere mei Deus quomiam conculcabit me homo:*

*If a woman is bleeding,[218] take a glass of wine and say this Psalm 7 times over it and give it to her to drink; she will be delivered. The Moon as above.*

## COMMENTARY:

The Latin in the title is the first half of verse two, *"Have mercy on me, O God, for man hath trodden me under foot"*.

*Sepher Shimmush Tehillim* advises this Psalm for those wishing to be liberated from sins of passion and lust.[219]

A similar use is seen in *A Treatise of Mixed Cabalah*, where verse five, *"In God I will praise my words, in God I have put my trust: I will not fear what flesh can do against me"*, is given against women's haemorrhages.[220]

Verse eleven, *"In God have I hoped, I will not fear what man can do to me"*, is written around the edge of a Lunar Pentacle which is used for protection when travelling by water (see Moon 2, Appendix 4).

218 Or haemorrhaging: presumably from childbirth: lit 'in a bleeding [state]'.
219 The Sixth and Seventh Books of Moses, Peterson, 2008:191.
220 A Collection of Magical Secrets, Skinner, Rankine & Barron, 2009:121.

# PSALM 56

**_Miserere mei Deus, miserere mei._**

*If you find yourself in a desert and you fear its ferocious beasts, recite this Psalm seven times and you will have naught to fear with the aid of God.*
*The Moon as above.*

*[200]*

## COMMENTARY:

The Latin in the title is the first part of verse two, *"Have mercy on me, O God, have mercy on me"*.

*Sepher Shimmush Tehillim* recommends using this Psalm to be fortunate in your undertakings, by reciting it daily after morning prayer in Church with the divine name Chi (ChI, *'Living'*).[221]

This is the last of the sequence of three Psalms (60, 52, 56) to be spoken over the candles to purify them prior to consecration in the *Key of Solomon*.[222]

---

221 The Sixth and Seventh Books of Moses, Peterson, 2008:191.
222 The Key of Solomon the King, Mathers, 1976:104.

# PSALM 57

*Si vere utique justitiam loquimini*

*If you wish to destroy the effects of an enchantment, recite this Psalm 7 times; no one will be able to harm you. It is also good against treacheries. The Moon as above.*

## COMMENTARY:

The Latin in the title is the first half of verse two, *"If in very deed you speak justice"*.

According to *Sepher Shimmush Tehillim*, if this Psalm is recited quickly when being attacked by a vicious dog, it will not harm you.[223]

Verses eleven and twelve, *"The just shall rejoice when he shall see the revenge: he shall wash his hands in the blood of the sinner. And man shall say: If indeed there be fruit to the just: there is indeed a God that judgeth them on the earth"*, are given in *A Treatise of Mixed Cabalah* for protecting yourself from wicked judges who persecute the poor.[224]

---

223 The Sixth and Seventh Books of Moses, Peterson, 2008:191.
224 A Collection of Magical Secrets, Skinner, Rankine & Barron, 2009:115.

# PSALM 58

*Eripe me de inimicis meis Deus meus:*

*If someone is too tightly tied up for him to sleep with his wife, write this Psalm on a piece of virgin paper along with the characters and read it out 7 times over it, then attach it to the thigh of the husband and he will be delivered.*

*If an enchanted man wishes to have relations with some woman, let this be written with these characters and recite it over him and bind it as above and he will be delivered from the charm.*

*The Moon in ♐ or in ♌ hour of ♃.*

## COMMENTARY:

The Latin in the title is the first half of verse two, *"Deliver me from my enemies, O my God"*.

The implication of being *'too tightly tied up'* would be either performance anxiety through stress, or magically induced impotence. Considering the second paragraph, it seems more likely that a magical cause is being suggested.

*Sepher Shimmush Tehillim* recommends the use of this Psalm to be free from all inclinations to sin or do evil. The Psalm from verse two to the end is prayed with its appropriate prayer and holy name of Paltiel (PLTIAL, *'Strong God, my Rescuer and Saviour'*) for three successive days.[225]

A sixteenth century German text (*Additional MS 35333*, 1508 CE) described writing the Psalm with characters on a piece of virgin parchment and wearing it around the neck for protection.[226]

---

225 The Sixth and Seventh Books of Moses, Peterson, 2008:191.
226 Binding Words, Skemer, 2006:86.

# PSALM 59

## *Deus repulisti nos & destruxistis nos: Ja.*

*If you are in bondage because of your affairs, write this Psalm with billy goat's blood and along with the characters and bury them under the hinge of the door while reading this Psalm and you will be fortunate.*

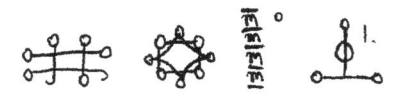

## COMMENTARY:

The Latin in the title is the beginning of verse three, *"O God, thou hast cast us off, and hast destroyed us"*. Ja occurs in the *Heptameron* as a divine name, and may be a contraction of Yah.

*Sepher Shimmush Tehillim* recommends that this Psalm should be recited with a suitable prayer and the divine name Yah (IH, *'God'*) for the safety of soldiers about to march into the battlefield.[227]

This is the fifth Psalm in the sequence of seven (3, 8, 30, 41, 59, 50, 129) for use in the preparation of the needle, burin and other iron instruments in the *Key of Solomon*.[228]

---

227 The Sixth and Seventh Books of Moses, Peterson, 2008:192.
228 The Key of Solomon the King, Mathers, 1976:115.

# PSALM 60

*Exaudi Deus deprecationem meam: Saday.*

*If you want to reconcile a husband with his wife, write these [201] characters with the blood of a white cockerel and read this Psalm 3 times over it and attach them to the arm of the woman; she will return.*

*The Moon in ↗ hour of Jupiter.*

## COMMENTARY:

The Latin in the title is the first half of verse two, *"Hear, O God, my supplication"*. Saday is a spelling of the divine name Shaddai (ShDI, *'Almighty'*, a divine name of the Sephira of Yesod on the Qabalistic Tree of Life).

According to *Sepher Shimmush Tehillim*, repeating this Psalm with the divine name Shaddai brings good fortune when one is about to take possession of a new dwelling.[229]

This is the first of the sequence of three Psalms (60, 52, 56) to be spoken over the candles to purify them prior to consecration in the *Key of Solomon*.[230]

---

229 The Sixth and Seventh Books of Moses, Peterson, 2008:192.
230 The Key of Solomon the King, Mathers, 1976:104.

# PSALM 61

*Nonne Deo subjecta erit anima mea? Jmoy.*

*Take some powder from under the altar when Mass is said and after the people have left. Read this Psalm over it seven times and scatter it in front of the house of your enemy. If he hates you, you will cut him down and his house will be destroyed.*

## COMMENTARY:

The Latin in the title is the first half of verse two, *"Shall not my soul be subject to God?"*

*Sepher Shimmush Tehillim* gives this Psalm for the forgiveness of all sins and transgressions. The Psalm is recited with the appropriate prayer whilst thinking of the divine name Itami (AITMI, *'Concealed, Hidden or Invisible'*) on Sunday immediately after evening prayer and on Monday after Vespers.[231]

Part of Verse eleven, *"if riches abound, set not your heart upon them"* is written around the edge of a Jupiterian Pentacle for discovering hidden treasure (see Jupiter 6, Appendix 5).

Verses eleven and thirteen, *"Trust not in iniquity, and cover not robberies: if riches abound, set not your heart upon them. and mercy to thee, O Lord; for thou wilt render to every man according to his works"*, are given in *A Treatise of Mixed Cabalah* for obtaining things necessary for living.[232]

---

231 The Sixth and Seventh Books of Moses, Peterson, 2008:192.
232 A Collection of Magical Secrets, Skinner, Rankine & Barron,

# PSALM 62

## *Deus Deus meus ad te de luce vigilo. Ja*

*Write this Psalm and attach it to a child's arm and he will cry no longer. The Moon as above.*

## COMMENTARY:

The Latin in the title is the first part of verse two, *"O God, my God, to thee do I watch at break of day"*. As mentioned for Psalm 59, Ja may be a contraction of Yah.

*Sepher Shimmush Tehillim* recommends repeating this Psalm whilst thinking of the divine name Yach (ICh) for a person wishing to withdraw from a firm, fearing they will be taken advantage of by their business partners and the resulting losses.[233]

Verses five and six, *"Thus will I bless thee all my life long: and in thy name I will lift up my hands. Let my soul be filled as with marrow and fatness: and my mouth shall praise thee with joyful lips"*, are given in *A Treatise of Mixed Cabalah* for a man to be rewarded with good things in his family.[234]

---

2009:115.
233 The Sixth and Seventh Books of Moses, Peterson, 2008:193.
234 A Collection of Magical Secrets, Skinner, Rankine & Barron, 2009:115.

# PSALM 63

*Exaudi Deus orationem meam cum deprecor*

*If anyone has any enemies, let him read out this Psalm and **Jubilate Deo** over the characters which he will have already written and let him attach them to his arm; he will overcome them.*

*The Moon in ♍ hour of ♃ or ☿.*

## COMMENTARY:

The Latin in the title is the first half of verse two, *" Hear, O God, my prayer, when I make supplication to thee"*.

*'Jubilate Deo'* is from Psalm 65.

A fourteenth century text (*Harley MS 2253*) advised the use of this Psalm as a textual amulet to be worn on the arm, using the same modus operandi, though the purpose was different (avoiding temptation).

*Sepher Shimmush Tehillim* advocates this Psalm for seafarers, wishing to complete their journey without accident and reach their destination in good health.[235]

This Psalm is the last of the four (81, 71, 133, 63) to be spoken over the silken cloth as part of its consecration, prior to its use for wrapping the instruments of the Art in the *Key of Solomon*.[236]

---

235 The Sixth and Seventh Books of Moses, Peterson, 2008:193.
236 The Key of Solomon the King, Mathers, 1976:116.

# PSALM 64

*Te decet Hymnus Deus in Sion. Ja.*

*If someone falls into need, let him read this Psalm seven times every [202] day and he will be delivered through the Grace of God.*

## COMMENTARY:

The Latin in the title is the first half of verse two, *"A Hymn, O God, becometh thee in Sion"*. As mentioned for Psalm 59, Ja may be a contraction of Yah.

A similar use is given in *A Treatise of Mixed Cabalah*, to acquire the fruits of the Earth in abundance, using verses twelve and thirteen, *"Thou shalt bless the crown of the year of thy goodness: and thy fields shall be filled with plenty. The beautiful places of the wilderness shall grow fat: and the hills shall be girded about with joy"*.[237]

Verses ten and eleven of the same work, *"Thou hast visited the earth, and hast plentifully watered it; thou hast many ways enriched it. The river of God is filled with water, thou hast prepared their food: for so is its preparation. Fill up plentifully the streams thereof, multiply its fruits; it shall spring up and rejoice in its showers"*, are given for making it rain at the appropriate time.[238]

---

237 A Collection of Magical Secrets, Skinner, Rankine & Barron, 2009:115.
238 Ibid, 2009:115.

In *Sepher Shimmush Tehillim*, there is a similar use, for fortune in all undertakings and obtaining the best results for petitions, combined with the divine name Yah (IH, *'God'*).[239]

239 The Sixth and Seventh Books of Moses, Peterson, 2008:193.

# PSALM 65

*Jubilate Deo omnis terra psalmum dicitur in nomine ejus.*

*If someone is poor and needy, let him read this Psalm seven times in the morning and seven times in the evening. His poverty will change into richness through God's permission.*

## COMMENTARY:

The Latin in the title is the end of verse one and the first half of verse two, *"Shout with joy to God, all the earth, sing ye a psalm to his name"*.

*Sepher Shimmush Tehillim* recommends this Psalm for dealing with possession by an evil spirit. The Psalm is written out on parchment and hung on the victim, and the hands stretched over him saying *"Save me, O God: for the waters are come in even unto my soul"* (Psalm 68:2).[240]

Verses four and five, *"Let all the earth adore thee, and sing to thee: let it sing a psalm to thy name. Come and see the works of God; who is terrible in his counsels over the sons of Adam"*, are given in *A Treatise of Mixed Cabalah* for praising God for the goods of the Earth, and thereby obtaining them more abundantly in future.[241]

---

240 The Sixth and Seventh Books of Moses, Peterson, 2008:193.
241 A Collection of Magical Secrets, Skinner, Rankine & Barron 2009:116.

# PSALM 66

## *Deus misereatur nostri & benedicat nobis: Ja.*

*Recite this Psalm over pure water and give it to a sick man to drink; he will be healed. Also write these characters and attach them to him.* ʒ ϩ ҄ 6 .

*The Moon in ♐ hour of ♃ .*

## COMMENTARY:

The Latin in the title is the beginning of verse two, *"May God have mercy on us, and bless us"*. As mentioned for Psalm 59, Ja may be a contraction of Yah.

This Psalm is the third of the five in the sequence for preparing the holy drink against elf influence and the devil's temptations in the Anglo-Saxon *Lacnunga* manuscript (C10th-11th CE).[242]

Again there is a possible root in *Sepher Shimmush Tehillim,* which recommends this Psalm with the divine name Yah (IH, *'God'*) for a protracted fever or severe imprisonment.[243]

Psalm 66 with its seven verses (not counting the opening reference to David) was often written on paper amulets in the form of a menorah, and King David was said to have done so on his battle shield.[244]

---

242 Leechcraft, Pollington, 2004:193.
243 The Sixth and Seventh Books of Moses, Peterson, 2008:193.
244 The Encyclopedia of Jewish Myth, Magic and Mysticism,

Verse eight of this Psalm has been found in Runic inscriptions for house blessing in a Psaltery found in Kävlinge, Sweden.[245]

This is the second in the sequence of three Psalms (2, 66, 53) to be spoken on entering a room or outdoor space for a ceremony before taking any action in the *Key of Solomon*.[246] It is also the second of the two Psalms spoken over the swallow or crow feather used to make a pen of the art in the *Key of Solomon*.[247]

Verses seven and eight, *"he earth hath yielded her fruit. May God, our God bless us, may God bless us: and all the ends of the earth fear him"*, are given in *A Treatise of Mixed Cabalah* to give thanks to God for the abundance of the Earth.[248]

Dennis, 2007:167.
245 Runic Amulets and Magic Objects, MacLeod & Mees, 2006:202.
246 The Veritable Key of Solomon, Skinner & Rankine, 2009:342.
247 The Key of Solomon the King, Mathers, 1976:109.
248 A Collection of Magical Secrets, Skinner, Rankine & Barron 2009:116.

# PSALM 67

*Exsurgat Deus & dissipentur inimici ejus. Ja*

*If you wish to prevent someone from sleeping, write this Psalm and bury it in front of his door.*
*If you also wish someone to stay, get close to him, look at him and say, **Exurgat Deus & dissipentur inimici ejus**. But if you wish him to withdraw, say, **& fugiant qui oderunt eum, a facie ejus.***

## ORATION

*Lord, The Master of all things who feedeth the Just with spiritual banquets in the joy of your friendship, impart Thy grace unto us, if it is pleasing unto Thee, we, who are Thy flock to [203] understand Thy spirit and to possess Thee at the right hand of Thy Father, Thou who art shared to all and every man, through our Lord Jesus Christ. So mote it be.*

## COMMENTARY:

The Latin in the title is the first half of verse two, *"Let God arise, and let his enemies be scattered"*. As mentioned for Psalm 59, Ja may be a contraction of Yah.

This Psalm is recommended by *Sepher Shimmush Tehillim* for the exorcism of an evil spirit. The Psalm is prayed in a low voice whilst thinking of the divine name Yah

(IH, *'God'*) and in the name of the patient over a bowl of water upon which the sun has never shone. The patient's body is then washed with the water.[249]

*Sepher Shimmush Tehillim* also recommends that this Psalm written on parchment along with Psalm 100 will give protection against the persecution of evil spirits and vindictive persons when worn.[250]

Psalm 67 is the last of the sequence of five Psalms (2, 53, 50, 46, 67) given in the *Key of Solomon* to be recited before or during the creation of the magic circle.[251]

This Psalm is one of those in the sequence of nineteen (130, 14, 101, 8, 83, 67, 71, 132, 112, 125, 45, 46, 21, 50, 129, 138, 48, 109, 52) recited for conjuration of the wax used in making the Pentacles in the *Key of Solomon*.[252]

Verse two, *"Let God arise, and let his enemies be scattered: and let them that hate him flee from before his face"*, is written around the edge of a Lunar Pentacle which is used for gaining dream oracles, and also to protect from night phantoms and summoning the souls of the dead (see Moon 5, Appendix 4). The same verse is also around a Mercurial Pentacle for luck in games and business, protection from robbers and dispelling or uncovering disloyalty (see Mercury 10, Appendix 5).

Verse twenty-three, *"The Lord said: I will turn them from Basan, I will turn them into the depth of the sea"*, is given in *A Treatise of Mixed Cabalah* against dangers of waters and the sea, and to be saved quickly from them.[253]

The same work gives an unusual use for verse two, with the first half of the verse being used to prevent serpents from moving, *"Let God arise, and let his enemies be scattered"*; and the second half to release them, *"and let them that hate him*

---

249 The Sixth and Seventh Books of Moses, Peterson, 2008:193.
250 Ibid, Peterson, 2008:193.
251 The Veritable Key of Solomon, Skinner & Rankine, 2008:286.
252 The Key of Solomon the King, Mathers, 1976:114.
253 A Collection of Magical Secrets, Skinner, Rankine & Barron 2009:116.

*flee from before his face".*[254]

A phrase based on verse three is written on pure wax in the *Abramelin*, *"Adonai, banish him away like you banish the smoke away – and as the wax dissolves in water, so should all the godless stand before God".* The wax is then placed on seven glowing coals, and as it melts a verse based on *Numbers 10:35* is spoken seven times.

The *'Paracelsian Charm'*, mentioned by Reginald Scot in 1583, ends with an abbreviated form of verse 2, as the last three words of the charm:

*"Omnes spiritu laudet domnum moson habent dusot propheates exurgat disipentur inimicus".*[255]

This was still being used as a house protection charm in Pendle Forest (Yorkshire) in 1920 by a farmer as an anti-witch charm, showing the popularity and durability of this charm.

---

254 Ibid, 2009:119.
255 Charm against Witches and Evil Spirits, Weeks, 1920:147.

# PSALM 68

## *Salvum me fac Deus:*

*If you are at sea in bad weather or in a storm,
read this Psalm; calm will come and you will be ferried
in safety to where you wish to go.*

## COMMENTARY:

The Latin in the title is the beginning of verse two, *"Save me, O God"*.

*Sepher Shimmush Tehillim* suggests this Psalm for the libertine, who has become a slave to his senses and evil habits and wishes to escape them. The Psalm is prayed over water and then the water drunk.[256]

Verse two, *"Save me, O God: for the waters are come in even unto my soul"*, is given as part of an exorcism cure with Psalm 66 in the *Sepher Shimmush Tehillim*.[257]

Verse twenty-four, *"Let their eyes be darkened that they see not; and their back bend thou down always"*, is one of the two verses used around a Solar Pentacle for operations of invisibility (see Sun 6, Appendix 4). The same verse is used around a derivative Mercurial Pentacle for the same purpose (see Mercury 7, Appendix 5).

In the *Key of Solomon* this Psalm is also used with a watery theme, as words spoken by the magician when bathing.[258]

---

256 The Sixth and Seventh Books of Moses, Peterson, 2008:194.
257 Ibid, Peterson, 2008:194.
258 The Veritable Key of Solomon, Skinner & Rankine, 2008:341.

# PSALM 69

## *Deus in adiutorium meum intende:*

*Write this Psalm onto a new piece of card with the name of the illness and perfume it with incense three or four times a day and night and read them for 15 days and the illness will be healed.*

## COMMENTARY:

The Latin in the title is the first half of verse two, *"O God, come to my assistance"*.

Verse two of this Psalm was used for healing in *London Hay MS 10391*, though what the cure was for is unknown due to the fragmentary nature of the text.[259]

This Psalm is recommended by *Sepher Shimmush Tehillim* for overcoming enemies.[260]

Verse two, *"O God, come to my assistance; O Lord, make haste to help me"* is written around the edge of two Martial Pentacles, for use against weapons of fire and other offensive and defensive devices (see Mars 2, Appendix 5), and for military expeditions and to charm firearms (see Mars 10, Appendix 5). It is also around the edge of a Jupiterian Pentacle for games of chance (see Jupiter 2, Appendix 5).

This Psalm was part of a cure for witchcraft given by a Yorkshire cunning-man, combined with *Matthew 10:4-42* and *Deuteronomy 28:15-25*.[261]

---

259 Ancient Christian Magic, Meyer & Smith, 1999:263.
260 The Sixth and Seventh Books of Moses, Peterson, 2008:194.
261 Cunning-Folk, Davies, 2003:62

# PSALM 70

## *In te Domine speravi, non confundar in æternam:*

*If you go to the Palace of Justice, say this Psalm before approaching the Judge and you will win your case.*

## COMMENTARY:

The Latin in the title is the second half of verse one, *"In thee, O Lord, I have hoped, let me never be put to confusion"*.

*Sepher Shimmush Tehillim* states that this Psalm has the power to liberate anyone from prison if prayed seven times a day.[262]

In the *Goetia*, there are three Shemhamphorash angels associated with verses of this Psalm. These are the twenty-eighth Sheahiah, with verse twelve, *"O God, be not thou far from me: O my God, make haste to my help"*;[263] the thirtieth angel Omael, with verse five, *"For thou art my patience, O Lord: my hope, O Lord, from my youth"*;[264] and the thirty-first angel Lekabel with verse sixteen, *"I will enter into the powers of the Lord: O Lord, I will be mindful of thy justice alone"*.[265]

---

262 The Sixth and Seventh Books of Moses, Peterson, 2008:194.
263 The Goetia of Dr Rudd, Skinner & Rankine, 2007:410.
264 Ibid, 2007:410.
265 Ibid, 2007:411.

# PSALM 71

## Deus judicium tuum Regi da: Ha.

*Write this Psalm in the name of whom you wish to have and with the name of her mother and attach it to your arm. You will be loved and cherished by her.*

*The Moon ♐ hour of ♃.*

*[204]*

## COMMENTARY:

The Latin in the title is the beginning of verse two, *"Give to the king thy judgement, O God"*. Ha occurs in conjurations in the *Heptameron.*

*Sepher Shimmush Tehillim* advocates this Psalm for finding favour and grace from all men, and the prevention of poverty. The Psalm and the divine name Aha (AH) are written on parchment and hung around the neck.[266]

Verse two is used in the second of two versions of the conjuration of the Prince of the Thumb found in *Munich CLM 849*, for obtaining information. The opening words of the verse, which begins, *"Give to the king thy judgment, O God: and to the king's son thy justice"*, are given to be recited whilst casting the third of the three circles.[267] We can assume at least the first half of the verse is used, as the manuscript was written by a priest who used shorthand forms of verses.

---

266 The Sixth and Seventh Books of Moses, Peterson, 2008:194.
267 Forbidden Rites, Kieckhefer, 1997:334.

Verse eight of this Psalm, *"And he shall rule from sea to sea, and from the river unto the ends of the earth"* is used around the outside of a Saturnian Pentacle, which is used for repressing the pride of spirits and against all adversity (see Saturn 2, Appendix 4).

Verse nine of this Psalm, *"Before him the Ethiopians shall fall down: and his enemies shall lick the ground"* is used around the outside of a Saturnian Pentacle which is used for striking terror into spirits and controlling them (see Saturn 1, Appendix 4). A derivative version of this Pentacle was also ascribed to the Sun (see Sun 8, Appendix 5). A Martial Pentacle to be fortunate for military purposes also uses this verse (see Mars 1, Appendix 5).

This Psalm is recited before cutting the Reed used for flaying animals to make parchment in the *Key of Solomon*.[268] It is the first of the three Psalms (71, 116, 133) used in the conjuration of the parchment in the *Key of Solomon*. [269] It is also one of those in the sequence of nineteen (130, 14, 101, 8, 83, 67, 71, 132, 112, 125, 45, 46, 21, 50, 129, 138, 48, 109, 52) recited for conjuration of the wax used in making the Pentacles in the *Key of Solomon*.[270] This Psalm is the second of the four (81, 71, 133, 63) to be spoken over the silken cloth as part of its consecration, prior to use for wrapping the tools in the *Key of Solomon*.[271]

Verses seven and eight of this Psalm, *"In his days shall justice spring up, and abundance of peace, till the moon be taken sway. And he shall rule from sea to sea, and from the river unto the ends of the earth"*, are given in *A Treatise of Mixed Cabalah* for gaining the affection of princes, lords and all men and being pleasing to them. [272]

The second half of verse twenty-three with verse twenty-

268 The Key of Solomon the King, Mathers, 1976:111.
269 Ibid, 1976:113.
270 Ibid, 1976:114.
271 Ibid, 1976:116.
272 A Collection of Magical Secrets, Skinner, Rankine & Barron, 2009:111.

four, *"and I am always with thee. Thou hast held me by my right hand; and by thy will thou hast conducted me, and with thy glory thou hast received me"*, are given in the same work for ensuring no person refuses you an honest answer. [273]

273 Ibid, 2009:111.

# PSALM 72

### Quam bonus Israel Deus

*Write this Psalm, attach it to your arm and you will obtain that, which you will ask for. The Moon as before this one.*

## ORATION

*Be graceful to us, Lord, and unite us to Thee and may we love Thee in the midst of our salvation and our feelings so that we may be worthy to sing Thy praises eternally in the presence of the Children of Zion, through our Lord Jesus Christ. So mote it be.*

## COMMENTARY:

The Latin in the title is part of verse one, *"How good is God to Israel"*.

A fourteenth century text (*Harley MS 2253*) advised the use of this Psalm as a textual amulet to be worn on the arm, using the same modus operandi, though for a different purpose, being healing.

This Psalm should be recited by a man who is fearful of being forced to deny his faith, while staying in a heathen and idolatrous land, according to *Sepher Shimmush Tehillim*.[274]

This Psalm is the seventh in the sequence of eight

---

274 The Sixth and Seventh Books of Moses, Peterson, 2008:194.

Psalms (8, 21, 27, 29, 32, 51, 72, 134) to be recited during the consecration of the Pentacles in the *Key of Solomon*. The Pentacle is held over the incense towards the rising sun and the Psalms recited with devotion.[275]

Verse twenty-one, *"For my heart hath been inflamed, and my reins have been changed:"* is used around the edge of a Venusian Pentacle to succeed in ventures of love (see Venus 5, Appendix 5).

275 The Veritable Key of Solomon, Skinner & Rankine, 2008:304.

# PSALM 73

## *Ut quid Deus repulisti in finem*

*Write this Psalm in the name of your enemy; write his name along with the characters and place it into the fire.*

*He will flee immediately.*
*The Moon as above.*

## COMMENTARY:

The Latin in the title is part of verse one, *"O God why hast thou cast us off unto the end"*.

Again the roots of this use may stem from *Sepher Shimmush Tehillim,* which advocates this Psalm to bring enemies to a terrible end if they persecute and oppress you.[276]

---

276 The Sixth and Seventh Books of Moses, Peterson, 2008:194.

# PSALM 74

### *Confitebimur tibi Deus: Raha*

*The one who recites it to you will be blessed by God and
delivered from bondage and from prison, as were St
John the Evangelist, St Thomas the Martyr[277] and
several others. You should say it every day, just as
Saint Jerome and St Augustine affirm.
If it is written at the day and hour of Jupiter on a fox's
skin – with the character and the name of the
Intelligence, it serves merchants' [205] profits well; you
should wrap it in some taffeta material, bound with gold
and carry it on you and recite the Psalm every day.*

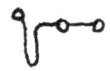

## COMMENTARY:

The Latin in the title is the beginning of verse two, *"We
will praise thee, O God"*. As the name of the intelligence is
not given in the text, the name Raha given in the heading is
almost certainly the relevant name.

This Psalm is recommended for the forgiveness of sins by
*Sepher Shimmush Tehillim.*[278]

St John the Evangelist (died circa 100 CE) is often
associated with St John the Apostle (although this is
debated), the author of the Gospel of John. Tradition holds

---

277 Probably St Thomas Becket.
278 The Sixth and Seventh Books of Moses, Peterson, 2008:194.

that St John was one of the original twelve apostles of Jesus and was the only one who lived into old age and was not killed for his faith. Some people also ascribe the *Book of Revelation* to St John, but this is also in doubt.

St Thomas Beckett was born in London in 1118 CE and later in life became the Archbishop of Canterbury. He was known to be in conflict over the rights and privileges of the Church (mainly to do with land taxes) with the monarch, Henry II and was assassinated in 1170 CE by the king's followers. He is buried in Canterbury cathedral in South East England.

St Augustine of Hippo was born in 354 CE in Thagaste, which is in modern-day Algeria. He is considered to be one of the most important philosophers and was extremely influential in the development of the Early Christian Church and was known to be heavily influenced by the Neo-Platonism of Plotinus. He was the one responsible for the doctrines of Original Sin and the Justification of War. He died in 430 CE in Hippo Regius (also in Algeria).

# PSALM 75

### *Notus in Judea Deus:*

*Write this Psalm at the waxing of the Moon and hang it from the door of a house, where there are Spirits and they will be dispelled.*

## COMMENTARY:

The Latin in the title is the first half of verse two, *"In Judea God is known"*.

This Psalm may be used for defence against dangers of fire and water according to *Sepher Shimmush Tehillim*.[279]

---

279 The Sixth and Seventh Books of Moses, Peterson, 2008:194.

# PSALM 76

### *Voce mea ad Dominum clamavi:*

*Write this Psalm on a glass plate then wash it in clean water, which you will give to drink to the person who has been bound to enchantments and he will be healed.*

## COMMENTARY:

The Latin in the title is the first half of verse two, *"I cried to the Lord with my voice"*

*Sepher Shimmush Tehillim* states that when this Psalm is prayed daily, no danger will touch you.[280]

Part of verse fourteen, *"who is the great God like our Elohim"* is used around the edge of a Martial Pentacle which is used for exciting war, discord and hostility, as well as resisting enemies and striking terror into rebellious spirits (see Mars 3, Appendix 4). In this a parallel to the destruction of enchantments described in the charm may be seen.

---

280 The Sixth and Seventh Books of Moses, Peterson, 2008:194.

# PSALM 77

*Attendite popule meus legem meam:*

*If you have any enemy, take a bronze drinking vessel and write this Psalm along with its characters inside this vessel, then fill it with clean water and say this Psalm over it 7 times and then pour it out in front of the door of your enemy.*

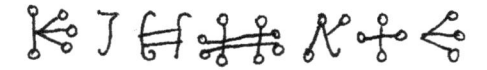

---

## COMMENTARY:

The Latin in the title is part of verse one, *"Attend, O my people, to my law"*.

In *Sepher Shimmush Tehillim*, this Psalm is used for receiving favour from kings and princes.[281]

---

281 The Sixth and Seventh Books of Moses, Peterson, 2008:194.

# PSALM 78

*Deus venerunt gentes in hereditatem tuam: Had*

*Write these characters on a new tablet and say this Psalm seven times over rose oil and wash these characters in it and then rub your face with it and you will be received honourably.*

[206]

## COMMENTARY:

The Latin in the title is part of verse one, *"O God, the heathens are come into thy inheritance"*.

*Sepher Shimmush Tehillim* states that when prayed, this Psalm is fatal to enemies and opponents.[282]

---

282 The Sixth and Seventh Books of Moses, Peterson, 2008:194.

# PSALM 79

## *Qui regis Israel, intende:*

*Write this Psalm on a new cooking pot along with these characters and fill it with clean water. Then say this Psalm seven times over it and wash a woman with the water and she will be chaste.*

*The Moon as above this one.*

---

## COMMENTARY:

The Latin in the title is the beginning of verse two, *"Give ear, O thou that rulest Israel"*.

One of the oldest known Psalm-based amulets, the lead scroll of Rodas from the first-third century CE, contains this Psalm.[283]

According to *Sepher Shimmush Tehillim*, this Psalm can help to save a man from falling into unbelief and from other errors.[284]

In the *Goetia*, the thirty-seventh Shemhamphorash angel, Aniel, is associated with verse eight of this Psalm, *"O God of hosts, convert us: and show thy face, and we shall be saved"*.[285]

---

283 The Septuagint in Context, Marcos & Watson, 2000:268.
284 The Sixth and Seventh Books of Moses, Peterson, 2008:194.
285 The Goetia of Dr Rudd, Skinner & Rankine, 2007:411.

# PSALM 80

*Exultate Deo adjutori nostro:*

*Write these characters on a leaf from an olive tree and perfume it with mastic and attach it to the arm of a sick man then read this Psalm and the haemorrhage will cease.*

## COMMENTARY:

The Latin in the title is the first half of verse two, *"Rejoice to God our helper"*.

According to *Sepher Shimmush Tehillim*, this Psalm can help to save a man from falling into unbelief and from other errors.[286]

This Psalm is the fourth in the sequence of five Psalms (17, 13, 54, 80, 117) to be recited whilst bathing before conjuration in the *Key of Solomon*.[287]

---

286 The Sixth and Seventh Books of Moses, Peterson, 2008:194.
287 The Veritable Key of Solomon, Skinner & Rankine, 2008:341.

# PSALM 81

## *Deus stetit in synagoga Deorum:*

*Write these characters and read this above Psalm and wash them with common oil or with rose oil and rub your face with it – you will be agreeably and honourably received.*

*The Moon as above this one.*

## COMMENTARY:

The Latin in the title is part of verse one, *"God hath stood in the congregation of gods"*.

*Sepher Shimmush Tehillim* recommends this Psalm may be used to help an employee perform his job to the satisfaction of his employers and to allow his business affairs to prosper and succeed.[288]

This Psalm is the first of the four (81, 71, 133, 63) to be spoken over the silken cloth as part of its consecration, prior to its use for wrapping the instruments of the Art in the *Key of Solomon*.[289]

In *A Treatise of Mixed Cabalah*, verses one and two, *"God hath stood in the congregation of gods: and being in the midst of them he judgeth gods. How long will you judge unjustly: and accept the persons of the wicked"*, are used for winning a law suit.

---

288 The Sixth and Seventh Books of Moses, Peterson, 2008:194.
289 The Key of Solomon the King, Mathers, 1976:116.

# PSALM 82

## *Deus quis similis erit tibi?*

*Take a new cooking pot and write the following characters in it; fill it with water, with which a woman has washed herself and read this Psalm over it seven times. Then pour it out in the house of your enemy and he will be destroyed.*

*The Moon as above this one.*
*[207]*

**COMMENTARY:**

The Latin in the title is the first half of verse two, *"O God, who shall be like to thee?"*

*Sepher Shimmush Tehillim* recommends this Psalm for being kept safe during war, avoiding defeat and captivity; though if captured, you will not be harmed. The Psalm should be written on parchment and hung around the neck.[290]

This is the first of the two Psalms spoken over the swallow or crow feather used to make a pen of the art in the *Key of Solomon*.[291]

---

290 The Sixth and Seventh Books of Moses, Peterson, 2008:194.
291 The Key of Solomon the King, Mathers, 1976:109.

# PSALM 83

*Quam dilecta tabernacula tua Domine virtutum:*

*If you wish to have access to a Prince, write this Psalm until **Respice in faciem Christi tui.** Bind it to your arm. You will be honourably received. The Moon as before this one.*

## COMMENTARY:

The Latin in the title is verse two, *"How lovely are thy tabernacles, O Lord of Hosts!"*

*Sepher Shimmush Tehillim* gives an interesting use for this Psalm. This Psalm with the divine name Av (AB, *'Father'*) are pronounced over a pot of water on which the sun has never shone, and the water poured over a person to banish bad smells acquired during a severe or protracted illness.[292]

This Psalm is one of those in the sequence of nineteen (130, 14, 101, 8, 83, 67, 71, 132, 112, 125, 45, 46, 21, 50, 129, 138, 48, 109, 52) recited for conjuration of the wax used in making the Pentacles in the *Key of Solomon*.[293]

This Psalm is the second of three written with some characters on a piece of virgin parchment and placed under the pillow for a dream vision of a thief and where he placed stolen goods.[294]

---

292 The Sixth and Seventh Books of Moses, Peterson, 2008:195.
293 The Key of Solomon the King, Mathers, 1976:114.
294 A Collection of Magical Secrets, Skinner, Rankine & Barron, 2009:23.

# PSALM 84

## *Benedixisti Domine terram tuam.*

*Write this Psalm on some laurel leaves and perfume it with mastic and with incense, mixed with rose oil and anoint your face with it. You will be fortunate and lucky. The Moon as above.*

## COMMENTARY:

The Latin in the title is the first half of verse two, *"Lord, thou hast blessed thy land"*.

*A Treatise of Mixed Cabalah* also gives a similar use to be lucky in all things, with verses twelve and thirteen, *"Truth is sprung out of the earth: and justice hath looked down from heaven. For the Lord will give goodness: and our earth shall yield her fruit"*.[295]

This Psalm is recommended by *Sepher Shimmush Tehillim* for reconciliation with a former friend. The Psalm and the divine name Vah (VH, the second half of Tetragrammaton) should be recited seven times facing south in an open field (note south is associated with wisdom in the Qabalah and in the *Talmud*).[296]

---

295 A Collection of Magical Secrets, Skinner, Rankine & Barron, 2009:116.
296 The Sixth and Seventh Books of Moses, Peterson, 2008:195.

# PSALM 85

## *Inclina Domine aurem tuam & exaudi me:*

*Read this Psalm twenty times over a wine press and write the characters and place them in the wine press. There will be blessings upon the wine.*

*The Moon as above.*

## COMMENTARY:

The Latin in the title is part of verse one, *"Incline thy ear, O Lord, and hear me"*.

This is the fifth of the five Psalms in the sequence for preparing the holy drink against elf influence and the devil's temptations in the Anglo-Saxon *Lacnunga* manuscript (C10th-11th CE).[297]

This Psalm is recommended by *Sepher Shimmush Tehillim* for frequent prayer to divert evil and attract good.[298]

---

297 Leechcraft, Pollington, 2004:193.
298 The Sixth and Seventh Books of Moses, Peterson, 2008:195.

# PSALM 86

## *Fundamenta ejus in montibus sanctis:*

*Write this Psalm along with the characters with the blood of a dove and perfume it with mastic and aloe wood; attach them to your arm and all your affairs will be soon fulfilled.*

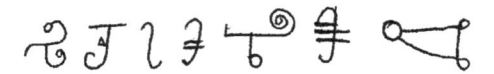

*The Moon and hour as before this one.*
*[208]*

## COMMENTARY:

The Latin in the title is the second half of verse one, *"The foundations thereof are in the holy mountains"*.

This Psalm is recommended by *Sepher Shimmush Tehillim* for frequent prayer to divert evil and attract good.[299]

---

299 The Sixth and Seventh Books of Moses, Peterson, 2008:195.

# PSALM 87

**_Domine Deus salutis meæ, in die clamavi, Saday._**

*If any enemy has harmed you in any thing, write this Psalm in a new cooking pot, filled with water from a well or a spring that has never seen the Sun nor the Moon and write these characters onto a glass plate and wash it with water, in which a woman will have washed; place this into the pot and pour it out at the door of your enemy, apart from that, also write these characters:*

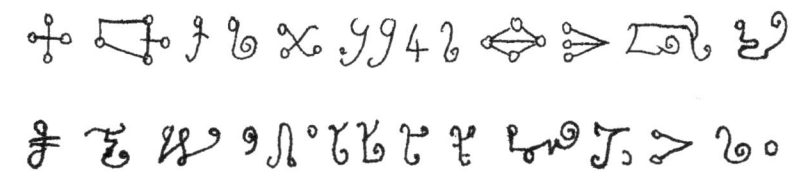

## COMMENTARY:

The Latin in the title is most of verse two, *"O Lord, the God of my salvation: I have cried in the day"*. Saday is a spelling of the divine name Shaddai (ShDI, *'Almighty'*, a divine name of the Sephira of Yesod on the Qabalistic Tree of Life).

This Psalm is recommended by *Sepher Shimmush Tehillim* for frequent prayer to divert evil and attract good.[300] It is also said to be especially good for the welfare of the community and the congregation.[301]

---

300 The Sixth and Seventh Books of Moses, Peterson, 2008:195.
301 Ibid, Peterson, 2008:195.

In the *Goetia* there are three Shemhamphorash angels associated with the verses of this Psalm. These are the sixteenth angel Hakamiah, with verse two *"O Lord, the God of my salvation: I have cried in the day, and in the night before thee"*;[302] the fortieth angel Yeiazel with verse fifteen *"Lord, why castest thou off my prayer: why turnest thou away thy face from me"*;[303] and the forty-third angel Vevaliah with verse fourteen *"But I, O Lord, have cried to thee: and in the morning my prayer shall prevent thee"*.[304]

302 The Goetia of Dr Rudd, Skinner & Rankine, 2007:410.
303 Ibid, 2007:411.
304 Ibid, 2007:411.

# PSALM 88

## *Misericordias Domini in æternam cantabo. Jad*

*Write this Psalm on the head of a person who has pain there and he will be delivered; read it also over holy water and sprinkle it in the house and God's blessing will be upon it.*

## COMMENTARY:

The Latin in the title is the first half of verse two, *"The mercies of the Lord I will sing forever"*. Jad may be a corruption of the Hebrew letter Yod, which like Aleph is often used as a shorthand for the divine.

A Similar use is given in *A Treatise of Mixed Cabalah*, with verse eighteen, *"For thou art the glory of their strength: and in thy good pleasure shall our horn be exalted"*, being given against headaches.[305]

*Sepher Shimmush Tehillim* recommends this Psalm for two diverse purposes. The first is for cases of severe and rapidly developing illnesses, where the Psalm is recited over olive oil and this poured onto ram's wool, which is used to anoint the patient's body. The second use is to liberate an arrested person, by going to an open field, raising your eyes to heaven and reciting the Psalm with a suitable prayer.[306]

---

305 A Collection of Magical Secrets, Skinner, Rankine & Barron, 2009:121.
306 The Sixth and Seventh Books of Moses, Peterson, 2008:195.

# PSALM 89

### *Domine refugium factus est nobis; Assas*

*It is suitable for acquiring wisdom and knowledge of mechanics and for succeeding in all ventures. It obtains benedictions from God through its prayers; it gives only blessings which must come and it cannot be prevented from arriving.*

*It removes charms and enchantments, which prevent a man from living with his wife. For that purpose, it is necessary to recite it and write it along with the [209] name of the Intelligence and the character on a piece of linen and always carry it around the neck and recite this Psalm morning and evening, every day and he will heal.*

## COMMENTARY:

The Latin in the title is part of verse one, *"Lord, thou hast been our refuge"*. The name Assas is almost certainly that of the intelligence mentioned in the text.

In *Sepher Shimmush Tehillim*, this Psalm is used in combination with the divine name Shaddai (ShDI, *'Almighty'*) for protection from lions and evil spirits or ghosts.[307]

This Psalm is one of those given by Rabbi Zacuto in a

---

307 The Sixth and Seventh Books of Moses, Peterson, 2008:195.

letter in 1672 CE as part of the exorcism process.[308]

In the *Goetia* the sixty-fifth Shemhamphorash angel, Damabiah, is associated with verse thirteen, *"Return, O Lord, how long? and be entreated in favour of thy servants"*.[309]

---

308 Between Worlds: Dybbuks, Exorcists, and Early Modern Judaism, Chajes, 2003:88.
309 The Goetia of Dr Rudd, Skinner & King, 2007:413.

# PSALM 90

### *Qui habitat in adjutori altissimi, Had.*

*Write this Psalm with the blood of a Dove and perfume it with roses and wood of aloe and carry it upon yourself; you will be preserved from Dæmons and protected from all enchantments, from thieves, ferocious beasts and from all manner of men, who lead wicked lives and if you travel by night, you will walk without fear. It is also good against children taking fright, if they carry it upon themselves.*

## COMMENTARY:

The Latin in the title is part of verse one, *"He that dwelleth in the aid of the most High"*.

This Psalm has a wide-ranging provenance for use in protection, being known as the *'Song Against Demons'*, with a history going back to the Apocryphal Psalms of the *Dead Sea Scrolls*, where a modified version is found in the leather scroll document 11Q11 dating to the late C1st BCE or early C1st CE. It is mentioned in the *Zohar* (C13th CE), which says, *"When the Sabbath departs, innumerable bands of evil spirits roam the world. The recitation of the Song against Demons was instituted to ward them off, lest Israel come under their control."*[310]

A variant form of verses one and two are found in the *Greek Magical Papyri* in PGM LXXXIII.1-20, *For fever with*

---

310 Zohar 1.14b.

*shivering fits.* The variant is, *"He who dwells in the help of the Most High shall abide in the shadow of the God of heaven. He will say of God, 'thou art my refuge and my help; I will put my trust in him.'"*311

A paraphrase of verse ten occurs in the Cairo Genizah 8 amulet (C4th-7th CE).312 It was popular in early Christian amulets, with verse two in a protective spell in *Berlin MS 9096*,313 verse one in an amulet to heal eye ailments (Berlin 21911, C5th CE)314 and verse ten in the text amulet Ianda 14 (C3rd-5th CE) for dæmonic protection.315 It was also used in an amulet given in *Sepher Razial* for protecting a mother and newborn child from sorcery, the Evil Eye and Dæmons.316

This Psalm was commonly combined with incipits from the Gospels in early Christian apotropaic charms, as seen in the papyrus amulet P. Vindob G348 from the C6th-7th CE. Other such examples include P. Oxy XVI (van Haelst 183), BKT VI vii 1 (van Haelst 731) and PSI VI 719.317

Recited forwards and backwards, this Psalm was thought to cure a person who had been injured by dæmonic attack (*Musayoff MS 219*, C17th CE).318 In *Sepher Shimmush Tehillim*, this Psalm is used in combination with the divine name Shaddai (ShDI, *'Almighty'*) for protection from lions and evil spirits or ghosts.319

The same work states that this Psalm is also good for a person possessed by an evil spirit and for a person afflicted by an incurable disease. It should be recited with the appropriate prayer and concentrating on the divine name El

311 The Greek Magical Papyri in Translation, Betz (ed), 1992:300.
312 Amulets and Magic Bowls, Naveh & Shaked, 1998:238-9.
313 Ancient Christian Magic, Meyer & Smith, 1999:34-5.
314 Ibid, 1999:32.
315 Ibid, 1999:46.
316 Sepher Rezial Hemelach, Savedow (ed), 2000:260.
317 See Catalogue des papyrus littéraires juifs et chrétiens, van Haelst, 1976 for more examples.
318 Between Worlds: Dybbuks, Exorcists, and Early Modern Judaism, Chajes, 2003:211.
319 The Sixth and Seventh Books of Moses, Peterson, 2008:196-8.

Shaddai (AL SHDI, *'Almighty God'*). It also recommends that if you write out this Psalm on parchment and conceal it behind the door of your house, you will be secure from evil accidents.[320]

Trachtenberg describes how the Psalm was recited before going to sleep to protect the speaker from being disturbed in the night, and how Rabbinic authorities such as Meir of Rothenburg and Jacob Weil would even recite it before taking a nap.[321] Additionally, because it did not contain the letter Zain (sword), it was used as a protection against weapons.[322]

Another use recorded by Trachtenberg was to confuse and dispel demons or evil spirits who might be following a funeral procession home after the ceremony. The procession stopped seven times, and each time recited the Psalm to verse 11, with one word of this latter verse (which contains seven words) being added at each stop.[323]

The first half of verse one, *"He that dwelleth in the aid of the most High"*, was frequently used as part of an apotropaic phrase painted on the lintels of doors belonging to Christian dwellings in Syria from the C4th CE.[324]

This power against demons is also seen with the use of Verse thirteen in the *Key of Solomon*. This verse, *"Thou shalt walk upon the asp and the basilisk: and thou shalt trample underfoot the lion and the dragon"*, is written around the edge of a Martial Pentacle for controlling demons, who cannot resist it (see Mars 5, Appendix 4). This verse is also used around two Solar Pentacles against venomous animals and poison, one of which is clearly derivative (see Sun 5 & Sun 6, Appendix 5). Verse thirteen is also used in the conjuration

---

320 The Sixth and Seventh Books of Moses, Peterson, 2008:199.
321 Jewish Magic and Superstition, Trachtenberg, 1939:116.
322 Ibid, 1939:116.
323 Ibid, 1939:180.
324 Magical Formulae on Lintels of the Christian Period in Syria, Prentice, 1906:144.

of Satan in *Munich CLM 849*.[325]

Verses eleven and twelve, *"For he hath given his angels charge over thee; to keep thee in all thy ways. In their hands they shall bear thee up:"* are used on a Solar Pentacle which is used for summoning spirits who can transport you great distances very quickly (see Sun 5, Appendix 4). A derivative Lunar Pentacle with the same verses was used for journeys by land or sea (see Moon 1, Appendix 5).

In the *Goetia*, two of the Shemhamphorash angels are associated with this Psalm. The third angel Sitael, is associated with verse two, *"He shall say to the Lord: Thou art my protector, and my refuge: my God, in him will I trust"*;[326] and the thirty-eighth angel Chaamiah, with verse nine, *"Because thou, O Lord, art my hope: thou hast made the most High thy refuge"*.[327]

This Psalm is also used as part of the preparation of a protective charm with Honesty herb (*lunaria annua*), also known as the Money Plant. The herb is plucked whole by the roots while reciting the Psalm and the seventy-two names of the Shemhamphorash. The charm may then be used to assist in acquiring treasure by nullifying the guardian spirits, rendering them harmless.[328]

In *A Treatise of Mixed Cabalah*, verses one and two, *"He that dwelleth in the aid of the most High, shall abide under the protection of the God of Jacob. He shall say to the Lord: Thou art my protector, and my refuge: my God, in him will I trust"*, are given to have God as your guardian.[329]

The same document gives verse three, *"For he hath delivered me from the snare of the hunters: and from the sharp word"*, as a protection against weapons.[330] Verses

---

325 Forbidden Rites, Kieckhefer, 1997:280.
326 The Goetia of Dr Rudd, Skinner & Rankine; 2007:408.
327 Ibid, 2007:410.
328 A Collection of Magical Secrets, Skinner, Rankine & Barron, 2009:42.
329 Ibid, 2009:116.
330 Ibid, 2009:117.

eleven and twelve, *"For he hath given his angels charge over thee; to keep thee in all thy ways. In their hands they shall bear thee up: lest thou dash thy foot against a stone"*, are given in this work to be safe during all journeys.[331]

Further examples from the same work include verses thirteen and fourteen, *"Thou shalt walk upon the asp and the basilisk: and thou shalt trample under foot the lion and the dragon. Because he hoped in me I will deliver him: I will protect him because he hath known my name"*, for protection from all beasts and serpents;[332] and verses fifteen and sixteen, *"He shall cry to me, and I will hear him: I am with him in tribulation, I will deliver him, and I will glorify him. I will fill him with length of days; and I will shew him my salvation"*, for conserving goods and honours in your life.[333]

An interesting use of the Psalm in the Old English *Lacnunga* manuscript (*Harley MS 585*, c.1000 CE) has verse ten, *"There shall no evil come to thee: nor shall the scourge come near thy dwelling"*, mixed with a quote from *Matthew 7:7* and some apparent gibberish with nine Pater Nosters in section twenty-five for curing black boils.[334]

---

331 Ibid, 2009:117.
332 Ibid, 2009:117.
333 Ibid, 2009:117.
334 Leechcraft, Pollington, 2003:191.

# PSALM 91

## *Bonum est confiteri Domino:*

*Write the Psalm on a new plate, washed with clean water and pour it out in the house of your enemy; God will prevent him from being able to do you harm.*

## COMMENTARY:

The Latin in the title is the first half of verse two, *"It is good to give praise to the Lord"*.

*Sepher Shimmush Tehillim* recommends this Psalm in order to attain high honours, high rank and increase good fortune. A sequence of Psalms (91, 93, 22, 19, 23, 99) should be pronounced three times in a row over a pot filled with new water and myrtle and grape leaves. Each time the person should wash himself with water from the pot, and anoint his face and body. He should then turn to face north and pray for the fulfilment of his desires (north is the direction of wealth in the Qabalah and the Talmud).[335]

This Psalm is the second of two given in the *Sepher Shimmush Tehillim* for use against an unyielding and bitter enemy, who causes great anxiety and pain (see Psalm 93 for more details).[336]

In the *Goetia*, the forty-seventh Shemhamphorash angel, Aushaliah, is associated with verse six of this Psalm, *"O Lord, how great are thy works! thy thoughts are exceeding*

---

335 The Sixth and Seventh Books of Moses, Peterson, 2008:200.
336 Ibid, Peterson, 2008:198-99.

*deep".*[337]

Verses eleven and thirteen of this Psalm are given in *A Treatise of Mixed Cabalah* for being named for worldly dignities. [338]

337 The Goetia of Dr Rudd, Skinner & Rankine, 2007:411.
338 A Collection of Magical Secrets, Skinner, Rankine & Barron, 2009:111.

# PSALM 92

## *Dominus regnavit decorum indutus est:*

*If you wish to bless a house, read this Psalm over holy water, write it out and bury it indoors and all the rats will flee.*

## COMMENTARY:

The Latin in the title is part of verse one, *"The Lord is clothed with strength"*.

*Sepher Shimmush Tehillim* recommends the proper use of this Psalm to win a law suit against an unjust opponent.[339]

---

339 The Sixth and Seventh Books of Moses, Peterson, 2008:200

# PSALM 93

## *Deus ultionem Dominus; Eleonetob.*

*Read this Psalm every day and all your enemies will flee; if you read it every day, it is also good [210] for the profit of a house or of a mill.*

## COMMENTARY:

The Latin in the title is the first half of verse one, *"The Lord is the God to whom revenge belongeth"*. The name Eleonetob in the heading is possibly a corruption of the divine name El Kano Tob (written Tob but pronounced Tov) used in *Sepher Shimmush Tehillim.*

*Sepher Shimmush Tehillim* gives this Psalm for use against an unyielding and bitter enemy, who causes great anxiety and pain. The procedure is to go to an open field on Monday, put some frankincense in one's mouth and turn to face towards the East and West and first recite Psalm 93, then Psalm 91 followed by an appropriate prayer, seven times, keeping in mind the divine name El Kano Tov (AL QNVA TVB, *'Great, strong, zealous and good God')*".[340]

This Psalm is one of those used in order to attain high honours, high rank and increase good fortune in *Sepher Shimmush Tehillim* (see Psalm 91 for more details).[341]

In the *Goetia* there are three Shemhamphorash angels associated with the verses of this Psalm. They are the fifteenth angel Hariel, with verse *"But the Lord is my refuge:*

---

340 The Sixth and Seventh Books of Moses, Peterson, 2008:200.
341 Ibid, Peterson, 2008:200.

*and my God the help of my hope*";[342] the thirty-third angel, Yechuiah, with verse eleven, *"The Lord knoweth the thoughts of men, that they are vain"*;[343] and the forty-fifth angel Saliah, with verse eighteen, *"If I said: My foot is moved: thy mercy, O Lord, assisted me"*.[344]

---

342 The Goetia of Dr Rudd, Skinner & Rankine, 2007:408.
343 Ibid, 2007:410.
344 Ibid 2007:410.

# PSALM 94

### *Venite exultemus Domino*

*If someone is possessed by a Dæmon, let him read this Psalm over a new tablet and let him wash it with holy water and holy oil. Anoint the sick man with it and he will be healed; write this Psalm and its characters and take care that he eats no billy goat meat.*

*The Moon as above.*

## COMMENTARY:

The Latin in the title is the first half of verse one, *"Come let us praise the Lord"*.

*Sepher Shimmush Tehillim* recommends this Psalm combined with the divine name El (AL, *'God'*, divine name of the Sephira of Chesed) for a pious believer to pray for his erring and unbelieving brethren.[345]

In the *Goetia*, the eighth Shemhamphorash angel, Kahetel, is associated with verse six of this Psalm, *"Come let us adore and fall down: and weep before the Lord that made us"*.[346]

---

345 The Sixth and Seventh Books of Moses, Peterson, 2008:201.
346 The Goetia of Dr Rudd, Skinner & Rankine, 2007:408.

# PSALM 95

## *Cantate Domino canticum novum*

*If rich people set traps for you, read this Psalm at the hour of Vespers seven times for three days and write it with the name of your Enemies. Attach it to your arm, then go forth boldly and make your requests.*

## COMMENTARY:

The Latin in the title is part of verse one, *"Sing ye to the Lord a new canticle"*.

*Sepher Shimmush Tehillim* advocates praying Psalms 95 and 96 together three times daily whilst contemplating the divine name Yah (IH, *'God'*), to provide great joy and contentment for the family.[347]

---

347 The Sixth and Seventh Books of Moses, Peterson, 2008:201.

# PSALM 96

*Dominus regnavit, exultet terra.*

*If you have a wife, whom you hate, write this Psalm
with musk, saffron, rosewater and some camphor then
perfume it with mastic and aloe wood and bury it in
front of her door and that for which you wish will come
to pass.*
*The Moon as above.*
*[211]*

## COMMENTARY:

The Latin in the title is part of verse one, *"The Lord hath
reigned, let the earth rejoice"*.

From the description the implication would be to make
an ink containing the musk, saffron, rosewater and
camphor.

*Sepher Shimmush Tehillim* advocates praying Psalms 95
and 96 together three times daily whilst contemplating the
divine name Yah (IH, *'God'*), to provide great joy and
contentment for the family.[348]

The *Abramelin* gives a prayer based on verse five for
bursting cliffs and stone in time of need. If chased by an
enemy and stopped by a cliff, the person should call three
times to Heaven, *"Adonai, Adonai, Adonai"*, and then with
outstretched hands hit the cliff whilst saying, *"The
mountains melt like wax in front of Adonai – the ruler of the*

---

348 The Sixth and Seventh Books of Moses, Peterson, 2008:201.

*whole earth"*. The book declares the person will then be amazed by the might of God and must take care to follow the second commandment.[349]

349 The Book of Abramelin, Worms, Dehn & Guth, 2006:63.

# PSALM 97

*Cantata Domino canticum novum. Ja*

*If you want to stop a ship that has its sails to the wind,[350] read this Psalm and it will stop.*

## COMMENTARY:

The Latin in the title is part of verse one, *"Sing ye to the Lord a new canticle"*. As mentioned for Psalm 59, Ja may be a contraction of Yah.

This Psalm is recommended by *Sepher Shimmush Tehillim* for establishing peace between families, with the divine name Yah (IH, *'God'*).[351]

In the *Goetia* there are two Shemhamphorash angels associated with verses of this Psalm., which are the thirteenth angel Yezalel, with verse four, *"Sing joyfully to God, all the earth; make melody, rejoice and sing"*;[352] and the forty-eighth angel Mihael, with verse two, *"The Lord hath made known his salvation: he hath revealed his justice in the sight of the Gentiles"*.[353]

---

350 I.e. is about to set sail.
351 The Sixth and Seventh Books of Moses, Peterson, 2008:201.
352 The Goetia of Dr Rudd, Skinner & Rankine, 2007:408.
353 Ibid, 2007:411.

# PSALM 98

### *Deus regnavit irascantur populi*

*Read this Psalm seven times in the morning and over water; wash your face with the water and you will be received honourably.*

**COMMENTARY:**

The Latin in the title is part of verse one, *"The Lord hath reigned, let the people be angry"*.

This Psalm should be used when you wish to become more pious according to *Sepher Shimmush Tehillim.*[354]

---

354 The Sixth and Seventh Books of Moses, Peterson, 2008:201.

# PSALM 99

## Jubilate Deo omnis terra.

*Against a mistress' hate, write this Psalm on a raw egg shell, place it in a glass of wine and let her drink it and she will love you.*

## COMMENTARY:

The Latin in the title is the beginning of verse two, *"Sing joyfully to God, all the earth"*.

*Sepher Shimmush Tehillim* recommends using this Psalm to overcome your enemies, by praying it seven times successively for seven days, whilst concentrating on the divine name Yah (IH, *'God'*).[355]

This Psalm is one of those used in order to attain high honours, high rank and increase good fortune in *Sepher Shimmush Tehillim*. The sequence is 91, 93, 22, 19, 23, 99 (see Psalm 91 for more details).[356]

In the *Goetia*, the sixty-third Shemhamphorash angel, Anuel, is associated with the second half of verse two of this Psalm, *"serve ye the Lord with gladness. Come in before his presence with exceeding great joy"*.[357]

---

355 The Sixth and Seventh Books of Moses, Peterson, 2008:201.
356 Ibid, Peterson, 2008:201.
357 The Goetia of Dr Rudd, Skinner & Rankine, 2007:412.

# PSALM 100

## *Misericordiam & Judicium*

*Write this Psalm along with the characters and bury them in the corners of your vineyard; no man will take any grapes from there without your permission. Write it also on a glass plate and wash it with holy water and read it seven times over the aforementioned water and give it to an enchanted man to drink and he will be healed.*

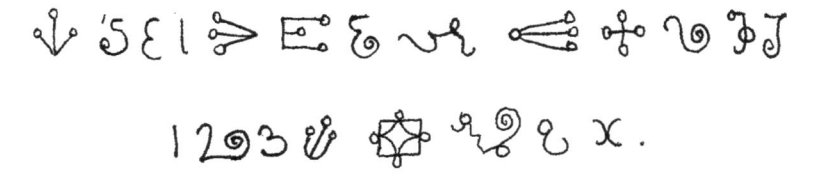

*The Moon as above.*
*[212]*

---

## COMMENTARY:

The Latin in the title is part of verse one, *"Mercy and judgement"*.

*Sepher Shimmush Tehillim* recommends that this Psalm written on parchment along with Psalm 67 will give protection against the persecution of evil spirits and vindictive persons when worn.[358]

---

358 The Sixth and Seventh Books of Moses, Peterson, 2008:201.

# PSALM 101

## Domine exaudi orationem meam: Ja

*Read this Psalm before leaving the house; you will find only joy and happiness.*

## COMMENTARY:

The Latin in the title is the first half of verse two, *"Hear, O Lord, my prayer"*. As mentioned for Psalm 59, Ja may be a contraction of Yah.

This Psalm used with the divine name Yah (IH, *'God'*) is said by *Sepher Shimmush Tehillim* to be good for helping barren women conceive.[359]

This is the fifth of the seven Penitential Psalms.

This Psalm is one of those in the sequence of nineteen (130, 14, 101, 8, 83, 67, 71, 132, 112, 125, 45, 46, 21, 50, 129, 138, 48, 109, 52) recited for conjuration of the wax used in making the Pentacles in the *Key of Solomon*.[360]

In the *Goetia*, the fifty-fifth Shemhamphorash angel, Mebahiah, is associated with verse thirteen of this Psalm, *"But thou, O Lord, endurest for ever: and thy memorial to all generations"*.[361]

---

359 The Sixth and Seventh Books of Moses, Peterson, 2008:202.
360 The Key of Solomon the King, Mathers, 1976:114.
361 The Goetia of Dr Rudd, Skinner & Rankine, 2007:411.

# PSALM 102

## *Benedic anima mea Domino; Ha*

*If someone languishes in sickness, read this Psalm seven times over common oil and rub the sick man with it and he will be healed.*

## COMMENTARY:

The Latin in the title is part of verse one, *"Bless the Lord, O my soul"*. Ha occurs in conjurations in the *Heptameron*.

This Psalm used with the divine name Aha (AH) is said by *Sepher Shimmush Tehillim* to be good for helping barren women conceive.[362]

In the *Goetia* the fifty-fourth Shemhamphorash angel Nithael, is associated with verse nineteen of this Psalm, *"The Lord hath prepared his throne in heaven: and his kingdom shall rule over all"*.[363]

In *A Treatise of Mixed Cabalah*, verses seven and eight, *"He hath made his ways known to Moses: his wills to the children of Israel. The Lord is compassionate and merciful: longsuffering and plenteous in mercy"*, are given for receiving God's wisdom.[364]

---

362 The Sixth and Seventh Books of Moses, Peterson, 2008:202.
363 The Goetia of Dr Rudd, Skinner & Rankine, 2007:411.
364 A Collection of Magical Secrets, Skinner, Rankine & Barron, 2009:117.

# PSALM 103

### *Benedic anima mea Domino*

*Write this Psalm on a Friday at dawn with the blood of a bat or that of a black hen onto the skin of a nanny-goat along with  your name and that of the woman, whom you desire, along with the name of her father and her mother and with these characters; it should all be written with a golden ink-pen; then take a new cooking pot, into which you place the skin, which has the names and the characters written on it; cover it with the type of earth, from which these sorts of pots or earthenware bowls are made; place them in the fire and while the skin burns, recite this Psalm seven times from the Easterly side on your knees. It is better to have bat's blood.*

*Otherwise, if you want to enflame the heart of any person, write this Psalm and the following characters with her [213] name and the name of her mother with a bronze or iron ink-pen and perfumed with mastic, galbanum and with aloe wood and place the parchment skin in a small earthenware vessel, sealed well with wax and place it in the fire and for the time being, just read the Psalm seven times over the fire and you will see some wonders.*

## COMMENTARY:

The Latin in the title is part of verse one, as with the previous Psalm, *"Bless the Lord, O my soul"*.

A similar use is found in *Sepher Razial*, where a spell for love and friendships is performed using a copper or bronze pen and ink made from lilies and crocuses. The Psalm was written out in full along with a set of characters in Angelic Script, which are however different to those given in this MS.[365]

*Sepher Shimmush Tehillim* declares that praying this Psalm frequently will destroy the Mazik (Jewish name for the Devil, referring here to the tendency to sin).[366]

In the *Goetia* the fifty-first Shemhamphorash angel, Hachashiah, is associated with verse thirty-one of this Psalm, *"May the glory of the Lord endure for ever: the Lord shall rejoice in his works"*.[367]

In *Munich CLM 849*, verse nine is used as part of a conjuration of the archangel Gabriel,[368] so it is interesting to see that this Psalm is also the second of two used in a technique of seeking answers from the appropriate planetary archangel of the day.[369]

365 Sepher Rezial Hemelach, Savedow (ed), 2000:269.
366 The Sixth and Seventh Books of Moses, Peterson, 2008:202.
367 The Goetia of Dr Rudd, Skinner & Rankine, 2007:411.
368 Forbidden Rites, Kieckhefer, 1997:298.
369 A Collection of Magical Secrets, Skinner, Rankine & Barron, 2009:97-8.

# PSALM 104

## Confitemini Domino & invocate, Vah.

*If anyone is held in prison too long, write this Psalm and attach it to his arm and let him read this Psalm during the day and he will be soon delivered.*

## COMMENTARY:

The Latin in the title is part of verse one, *"Give glory to the Lord, and call upon his name"*. Vah may be a corruption of Vau, the sixth letter of the Hebrew alphabet and third in the Tetragrammaton (IHVH).

*Sepher Shimmush Tehillim* suggests praying the Psalm with the divine name Yah (IH, *'God'*) to cure the three day fever.[370]

Verses 32-3, *"He gave them hail for rain, a burning fire in the land. And he destroyed their vineyards and their fig trees:"* are used around the edge of a Martial Pentacle for creating hail and tempest (see Mars 7, Appendix 4).

---

370 The Sixth and Seventh Books of Moses, Peterson, 2008:202.

# PSALM 105

## *Confitemini Domino quoniam bonus. Ja*

*If you wish to sink a sailing ship, read this Psalm seven
times over salt and throw it onto the boat, where the
sails have been spread and it will be sunk.*

## COMMENTARY:

The Latin in the title is part of verse one, *"Give glory to
the Lord, for he is good"*. As mentioned for Psalm 59, Ja may
be a contraction of Yah.

*Sepher Shimmush Tehillim* suggests praying the Psalm
with the divine name Yah (IH, *'God'*) to cure the four day
fever.[371]

The water connection with this Psalm is seen elsewhere,
as in the *Key of Solomon*, where this is one of the Psalms
spoken during bathing for purification.[372]

In the *Goetia*, the sixty-eighth Shemhamphorash angel,
Chabuiah, is associated with verse one of this Psalm, *"Give
glory to the Lord, for he is good: for his mercy endureth for
ever"*.[373]

A very different use is seen in *A Treatise of Mixed
Cabalah*, where verse four, *"Remember us, O Lord, in the
favour of thy people: visit us with thy salvation"*, is given
against malaria.[374]

---

371 The Sixth and Seventh Books of Moses, Peterson, 2008:202.
372 The Veritable Key of Solomon, Skinner & Rankine, 2008:341.
373 The Goetia of Dr Rudd, Skinner & Rankine, 2007:411.
374 A Collection of Magical Secrets, Skinner, Rankine & Barron,
2009:122.

# PSALM 106

## *Confitemini Domino quoniam bonus. Vau*

*If your enemy is in prison and you would wish him to be there for a long time, go to the prison and read this Psalm in front of him and he will not get out of there for a long time.*
*[214]*

## COMMENTARY:

The Latin in the title is the first half of verse one, and again repeats the preceding Psalm words, *"Give glory to the Lord, for he is good"*. Vau is the sixth Hebrew letter, associated with the Son as the third part of Tetragrammaton.

*Sepher Shimmush Tehillim* suggests praying the Psalm with the divine name Yah (IH, *'God'*) to cure the daily fever.[375]

Verse 16, *"Because he hath broken gates of brass, and burst the iron bars"*, is written around the edge of a Lunar Pentacle which is for summoning Lunar spirits, and opening doors (see Moon 1, Appendix 4).

A similar theme is seen in the *Abramelin*, where prayers based on verses of this Psalm are used to escape if locked between iron doors by an enemy. The person is advised to fall to their knees and call fervently to Adonai, then go to the gateway and say the prayer (based on verse fifteen) seven times in different ways, *"Adonai we want to thank you for the*

---

375 The Sixth and Seventh Books of Moses, Peterson, 2008:202.

*grace and wonders that you show to humankind"*. Next write or scratch the words *"Remember David and his promise"* below the door, or with spit and the right index finger. Under this write *"Yah"* and *"He breaks armoured doors and removes rivets from iron"* (based on verse sixteen), and then strike the door seven times. As the door opens, before leaving say a prayer based on verse one, *"We who are released by Adonai, and those who have been saved from their need should say, 'Praise Adonai because he is merciful and his grace lasts eternity.'"*[376]

---

376 The Book of Abramelin, Worms, Dehn & Guth, 2006:64-5.

# PSALM 107

*Paratum cor meum Deus, paratum cor meum:*

*If you wish to approach a Prince or a King, read this Psalm seven times before entering and you will have naught to fear.*

## COMMENTARY:

The Latin in the title is the first half of verse two, *"My heart is ready, O God, my heart is ready"*.

According to *Sepher Shimmush Tehillim*, this Psalm written upon clean parchment with the divine name Vi (VI, two of the letters from Jahveh, the Tetragrammaton) and hidden behind the door of the house will bless all comings and goings and ensure business transactions will be successful.[377]

---

377 The Sixth and Seventh Books of Moses, Peterson, 2008:202.

# PSALM 108

### Deus laudem meam ne tacueris

*Write this Psalm until* **Et qui loquuntur mala adversus animam meam** *and wash it with water, in which women have bathed on a Saturday and sprinkle the water in the house of your enemy. The memory of him will be erased from the surface of the Earth.*

## COMMENTARY:

The Latin in the title is the first part of verse two, *"O God, be not thou silent in thy praise"*.

There is an early precedent for such a use of this Psalm, in an early Syriac Psalter which advocated putting mustard seed and water in a new pot, reading the Psalm over it for three days and then pouring it on the enemy's doorstep to kill him.[378]  This is clearly the basis of the use in *Sepher Shimmush Tehillim*, and probably the derivative version in *Le Livre d'Or*.

*Sepher Shimmush Tehillim* recommends this Psalm to vanquish a mighty and oppressive enemy.  A new jug is filled with new sparkling wine and some mustard added to it. The Psalm is repeated over it for three days successively, while thinking on the divine name El (AL, *'God'*). The mixture is then poured before the door of the enemy's house, making

---

378 Magic and Ritual in the Ancient World, Mirecki & Meyer, 2002:441.

sure not to spill any on oneself.[379]

This use is continued in the *Key of Solomon* usage of this Psalm. Verse 18, *"And he loved cursing, and it shall come unto him: and he would not have blessing, and it shall be far from him. And he put on cursing, like a garment: and it went in like water into his entrails, and like oil in his bones"* is used around the edge of a Saturnian Pentacle which is used for bringing destruction or ruin, or alternatively news of a particular event or person (see Saturn 4, Appendix 4).

Verse 6, *"Set thou the sinner over him: and may the devil stand at his right hand"* is used on a Saturnian Pentacle for obsessing a person with madness and demons (see Saturn 6, Appendix 4). A later version of the same Saturnian Pentacle is seen in other manuscripts (see Saturn 5, Appendix 5).

In the *Goetia*, the seventy-first Shemhamphorash angel, Hayiel, is attributed to this Psalm, *"I will give great thanks to the Lord with my mouth: and in the midst of many I will praise him"*.[380]

---

379 The Sixth and Seventh Books of Moses, Peterson, 2008:202.
380 The Goetia of Dr Rudd, Skinner & Rankine, 2007:412.

# PSALM 109

## *Dixit Dominus Domino meo:*

*Write the Psalm until **ex utero ante luciferum genui te** and attach it to the right thigh of a pregnant woman and she will give birth immediately.*

## COMMENTARY:

The Latin in the title is the opening of verse one, *"The Lord said to my Lord"*.

This Psalm in combination with the divine name Yah (IH, 'God') is given by *Sepher Shimmush Tehillim* to compel an enemy or an adversary to grovel, ask for forgiveness and make peace.[381]

Verse 5, *"The Lord at thy right hand hath broken kings in the day of his wrath"* is written around the edge of a Martial Pentacle used for gaining victory in war (see Mars 4, Appendix 4). A derivative Martial Pentacle for military expeditions and against bad encounters is seen in other manuscripts (see Mars 4, Appendix 5).

This Psalm is one of those in the sequence of nineteen (130, 14, 101, 8, 83, 67, 71, 132, 112, 125, 45, 46, 21, 50, 129, 138, 48, 109, 52) recited for conjuration of the wax used in making the Pentacles in the *Key of Solomon*.[382]

---

381 The Sixth and Seventh Books of Moses, Peterson, 2008:203.
382 The Key of Solomon the King, Mathers, 1976:114.

# PSALM 110

*Confitebor tibi Domine in toto corde meo:*

*Read this Psalm where you wish to build and the place will be blessed.*

## COMMENTARY:

The Latin in the title is the first half of verse one, *"I will praise thee, O Lord, with my whole heart"*.

*Sepher Shimmush Tehillim* gives this Psalm in order to acquire many friends.[383]

---

383 The Sixth and Seventh Books of Moses, Peterson, 2008:203.

# PSALM 111

## Beatus vir qui timet Dominum:

*Take some powdered swallow and for three days, [215] read this Psalm over it until* **Donec despiciat inimicos suos** *and scatter it in the house of your enemy and he and all that is of him will perish.*

## COMMENTARY:

The Latin in the title is the first half of verse one, *"Blessed is the man that feareth the Lord"*.

The opposite use is seen in *Abramelin*, with a prayer based on the first three verses being scratched onto a clean seven-sided building block that has never been wet with a new gold or silver stylus as part of a rite to keep a house safely protected from misfortune. The prayer is, *"Blessed be the one who fears God and finds pleasing his commandments. He will have surplus and abundance and his righteousness will be carried forever in his seed."* Afterwards the stone is fumigated seven times and buried one ell under the house. At the next three new moons incense is burned where the stone is buried.[384]

This Psalm is used to increase might and power according to *Sepher Shimmush Tehillim*.[385]

Mathers wrote that Verse 3, *"Glory and wealth shall be in his house: and his justice remaineth for ever and ever"*, was

---

384 The Book of Abramelin, Worms, Dehn & Guth, 2006:65-6.
385 The Sixth and Seventh Books of Moses, Peterson, 2008:203.

implied in the letters around the Hexagram in a Jupiterian Pentacle for acquiring glory, riches and tranquillity of mind, and for discovering treasure and chasing away the guardian spirits (see Jupiter 2, Appendix 4).[386]   This verse is also found around the edge of another Jupiterian Pentacle which is for acquiring riches and honour (see Jupiter 4, Appendix 4) and is also seen on a similar Solar Pentacle (see Sun 1, Appendix 5).

---

386 For more on this see The Book of Treasure Spirits, Rankine, 2009.

# PSALM 112

### *Laudate pueri Dominum*

*Read this Psalm over holy water and sprinkle your house with it seven times; all that you will receive will be profitable:*
*It is also very good written down and placed in a stable for the protection of sheep, cattle and goats.*

## COMMENTARY:

The Latin in the title is the first half of verse one, *"Praise the Lord, ye children"*.

*Sepher Shimmush Tehillim* recommends this Psalm to check growing heresy and infidelity.[387]

Verses 7-8, *"Raising up the needy from the earth, and lifting up the poor out of the dunghill: That he may place him with princes, with the princes of his people"* are written around the edge of a Jupiterian Pentacle which is used for protection from poverty, as well as discovering treasure and driving away guardian treasure spirits (see Jupiter 7, Appendix 4). A derivative Solar Pentacle for honour and riches uses the same verses (see Sun 2, Appendix 5).

This Psalm is one of those in the sequence of nineteen (130, 14, 101, 8, 83, 67, 71, 132, 112, 125, 45, 46, 21, 50, 129, 138, 48, 109, 52) recited for conjuration of the wax

---

387 The Sixth and Seventh Books of Moses, Peterson, 2008:203.

used in making the Pentacles in the *Key of Solomon*.[388]

In the *Goetia*, two of the Shemhamphorash angels are associated with verses of this Psalm. These are the fifty-ninth angel Harachel, with verse three *"From the rising of the sun unto the going down of the same, the name of the Lord is worthy of praise"*;[389] and the sixty-first angel Umabel, with verse two *"Blessed be the name of the Lord, from henceforth now and forever"*.[390]

Verses seven and eight, *"Raising up the needy from the earth, and lifting up the poor out of the dunghill: That he may place him with princes, with the princes of his people"*, are given in *A Treatise of Mixed Cabalah* for rising up out of poverty and being raised up in honour and riches.[391]

A charm for fertility is given in the *Abramelin*, where this Psalm is read seven times over a glass of milk which has had a little fine incense thrown over it. The milk is given to the women before breakfast every day for a week. On the first day a tablet of gold, silver or pure beeswax is hung on her, which has been fumigated and with a verse based on verse two written on it, *"Praised is the name of Adonai, from now to eternity"* and with a prayer adapted from verse nine on the reverse, *"He who lets the unfertile live in the house and become the one who gives joy to children – hallelujah."*[392]

---

388 The Key of Solomon the King, Mathers, 1976:114.
389 The Goetia of Dr Rudd, Skinner & Rankine, 2007:411.
390 Ibid, 2007:412.
391 A Collection of Magical Secrets, Skinner, Rankine & Barron, 2009:118.
392 The Book of Abramelin, Worms, Dehn & Guth, 2006:56.

# PSALM 113

## In exitu Israël de Ægypto: Ha.

*Read this Psalm over holy water and spill it into fishermen's boats, skiffs or sailing ships and they will not be able to catch anything in their nets.*

## COMMENTARY:

The Latin in the title is the first half of verse one, *"When Israel went out of Egypt"*. Ha occurs in conjurations in the *Heptameron.*

A formula based on verses twelve to fifteen is used in an eighth century Christian text (*Berlin MS 8503*), *Abdallah's curses to weaken Mouflehalpahapani*, likening the victim to an idol and describing his condition, *"has hands but he cannot touch; he has feet but he cannot walk; he has eyes but he cannot see; he has ears but he cannot hear; he has a nose but he cannot smell; he has a mouth but he cannot speak a word through his throat; he has a heart but he does not understand"*.[393]

According to *Sepher Shimmush Tehillim*, if this Psalm is written on parchment with the divine name Aha (AH) and carried on the person it will bring success in business.[394]

In the *Goetia*, the fifty-seventh Shemhamphorash angel, Nemmamiah, is associated with verse nineteen of this Psalm, *"They that fear the Lord hath hoped in the Lord: he is their helper and their protector"*.[395]

---

393 Ancient Christian Magic, Meyer & Smith, 1999:201.
394 The Sixth and Seventh Books of Moses, Peterson, 2008:203.
395 The Goetia of Dr Rudd, Skinner & Rankine, 2007:411.

# PSALM 114

*Dilexi quoniam exaudiet Dominus vocem orationis meæ.*

*Write this Psalm until **Custodiens parvulos Dominus** and perfume it with mastic, musk and wood of aloe and attach it to the right arm of a child and he will be delivered form all manner of sicknesses and perils. The Moon in ⚹ hour of ♃*

## COMMENTARY:

The Latin in the title is verse one, *"I have loved, because the Lord will hear the voice of my prayer"*.

This Psalm has a contentious use in *Sepher Shimmush Tehillim*, which recommends praying this Psalm if one is determined to dispute and debate with infidels, heretics and scoffers at religion.[396]

In the *Goetia*, two of the Shemhamphorash angels are associated with verses of this Psalm. These are the thirty-fifth angel Kevaqiah, with verse one *"I have loved, because the Lord will hear the voice of my prayer"*;[397] and the seventy-second angel Mumiah, to verse seven *"Turn, O my soul, into thy rest: for the Lord hath been bountiful to thee"*.[398]

---

396 The Sixth and Seventh Books of Moses, Peterson, 2008:203.
397 The Goetia of Dr Rudd, Skinner & Rankine, 2007:410.
398 Ibid, 2007:412.

# PSALM 115

## *Credidi propter quod locutus sum:*

*Read this Psalm seven times over wine, which you are going to drink and you [216] will not become drunk at all and with it you will heal all those who also drink it. Also read this Psalm is you wish to approach a Prince or enter into a Council chamber and write it along with these characters and carry them with you and you will achieve what you wish.*

## COMMENTARY:

The Latin in the title is the first half of verse one, *"I have believed, therefore I have spoken"*.

This Psalm is recited three times as part of a charm for healing a horse with a sprain in the Anglo-Saxon *Lacnunga* manuscript (C10th-11th CE).[399]

This Psalm prayed daily is good against sudden or violent death, according to *Sepher Shimmush Tehillim.*[400]

Verses 7-8, *"Thou hast broken my bonds: I will sacrifice to thee the sacrifice of praise, and I will call upon the name of the Lord"* are written around the edge of a Solar Pentacle for release from imprisonment or iron fetters (see Sun 7, Appendix 4). A derivative Solar Pentacle is seen in other

---

399 Leechcraft, Pollington, 2003:235.
400 The Sixth and Seventh Books of Moses, Peterson, 2008:203.

manuscripts (see Sun 12, Appendix 5), with a similar derivative Mercurial Pentacle for protection against slavery and prison (see Mercury 1, Appendix 5).

# PSALM 116

### *Laudate Dominum omnes gentes*

*St Augustine says that it is good for destroying idleness
of lazy people, so that they may take pleasure in work.
It is also good for an innocent person, who is being
persecuted and for prisoners.*
*It is necessary to write its character on virgin parchment
and at sunset, hold it in your hand and staring at it,
recite the Psalm along with the name of the Intelligence,
then say the following Prayer.*
*Intelligence:* **Custel**

*Character:*

## PRAYER

*Lord of Truth, who knowest mine innocence, illuminate
the spirit of the one, who is to judge me in such a
manner that I may be freed and absolved.*

## COMMENTARY:

The Latin in the title is the first half of verse one, *"O
praise the Lord, all ye nations"*. The intelligence Custel is not
mentioned in other grimoires.

*Sepher Shimmush Tehillim* states that this Psalm is good
for repentance over broken vows and promises to do good

works.[401]

This is the second of the three Psalms (71, 116, 133) used in the conjuration of the parchment in the *Key of Solomon.* [402]

401 The Sixth and Seventh Books of Moses, Peterson, 2008:203.
402 The Key of Solomon the King, Mathers, 1976:113.

# PSALM 117

*Confitemini Domino quoniam bonus:*

*If you have lost the key of your room or house and you wish to return to them, read this Psalm seven times and the room or house will all be opened immediately.*
*[217]*

## COMMENTARY:

The Latin in the title is the first half of verse one, *"Give praise to the Lord, for he is good"*.

This is another Psalm which *Sepher Shimmush Tehillim* declares is good for silencing all free-thinkers, heretics and scoffers of religion, who wish to lead you astray.[403]

This Psalm is the last in the sequence of five Psalms (17, 13, 54, 80, 117) to be recited whilst bathing before conjuration in the *Key of Solomon*.[404]

Verse 6, *"The Lord is my helper, I will not fear what man can do unto me"* is written around the edge of a Martial Pentacle to be invulnerable (see Mars 3, Appendix 5).

Verses thirteen, sixteen and seventeen, *"Lord I have hated the unjust: and have loved thy law. Uphold me according to thy word, and I shall live: and let me not be confounded in my expectation. Help me, and I shall be saved: and I will meditate always on thy justifications"*, are recited over the perfumes thrown on the fire in the *Universal*

---

403 The Sixth and Seventh Books of Moses, Peterson, 2008:203.
404 The Veritable Key of Solomon, Skinner & Rankine, 2008:341.

*Treatise of the Keys of Solomon.*[405]

Part of Verse 16, *"The right hand of the Lord hath wrought strength: the right hand of the Lord hath exulted me:"* is written around the edge of a Mercurial Pentacle for games of chance (see Mercury 5, Appendix 5). It is also used as part of the conjuration of the Princes of the Thumb in the sixteenth century text *Codex Gaster 315.*[406]

A further use of this verse is seen on a twelfth century church bell from Gjerpen in Norway, where it was inscribed in Runes.[407]

The *Abramelin* gives the use of several verses of this Psalm for all sorts of sickness and disease. First the words of verse seventeen, *"I shall not die, but live: and shall declare the works of Adonai"*, are written in honey on seven clean glass bowls before sunrise. Then take seven small biscuits or breads and write the same verse on them. Fumigate one with the words of verses one and eighteen, *"Give praise to Lord, for he is good: for his mercy endureth for ever. The Lord chastising hath chastised me: but he hath not delivered me over to death"*. The fumigated bread and one of the clean bowls with water in should be given to the sick person as their first food of the day, not ignoring their other medicines. The biscuit should be eaten in seven bites.[408]

405 Ibid, 2008:390.
406 Babylonian Oil Magic, Daiches, 1913:15.
407 Runic Amulets and Magic Objects, MacLeod & Mees, 2006:199.
408 The Book of Abramelin, Worms, Dehn & Guth, 2006:47-8.

# PSALM 118

## *Beati immaculate in via:*

*Write this Psalm and read it seven times; perfume it with mastic and carry it on you and you will be protected from all infirmities. The Moon in ♐ hour of ♃.*

## COMMENTARY:

The Latin in the title is the first half of verse one, *"Blessed are the undefiled in the way"*.

*Sepher Shimmush Tehillim* gives numerous different uses for this, the longest Psalm. It is broken down into twenty-two divisions, each of eight verses corresponding to a Hebrew letter listed alphabetically, each of which has a different use, listed in Appendix 3.[409]

In the *Goetia*, there are four Shemhamphorash angels associated with verses of this Psalm. They are the twenty-sixth angel Haaiah, with verse one hundred and forty-five, *"I cried with my whole heart, hear me, O Lord: I will seek thy justifications"*;[410] the forty-fourth angel Yelahiah, with verse one hundred and eight, *"The free offerings of my mouth make acceptable, O Lord: and teach me thy judgments"*;[411] the fifty-third angel Nanael, with verse seventy-five, *"I know, O Lord, that thy judgments are equity: and in thy truth thou hast*

---

409 The Sixth and Seventh Books of Moses, Peterson, 2008:204-8.
410 The Goetia of Dr Rudd, Skinner & Rankine, 2007:409.
411 Ibid, 2007:410.

*humbled me"*;[412] and the sixty-second angel Yahahel, with verse one hundred and fifty-nine, *"Behold I have loved thy commandments, O Lord; quicken me thou in thy mercy"*.[413]

---

412 Ibid, 2007:411.
413 Ibid, 2007:412.

# PSALM 119

## *Ad Dominum cum tribularer clamavi*

*Read this Psalm seven times over water, in which a woman has washed herself on a Saturday and sprinkle it over the door of your enemy and he will flee and perish.*

## COMMENTARY:

The Latin in the title is the first half of verse one, *"In my trouble I cried to the Lord"*.

*Shimmush Tehillim* gives two uses for this Psalm. The first is to receive grace and favour, when it should be repeated before appearing before a Judge. The second is to pray the Psalm seven times when coming in sight of a forest, to be able to enter safely even if it is infested with poisonous snakes, scorpions and other poisonous creatures.[414]

In the *Goetia* two Shemhamphorash angels are associated with verses of this Psalm. They are the twentieth angel Pahaliah, with the first half of verse two *"O Lord deliver my soul"*[415] added to the phrase *"I shall call upon the name of the Lord,"*; and the whole of verse two, *"O Lord, deliver my soul from wicked lips, and a deceitful tongue"*,[416] being associated with the forty-first angel, Hahahel.

---

414 The Sixth and Seventh Books of Moses, Peterson, 2008:208.
415 The Goetia of Dr Rudd, Skinner & Rankine, 2007:409.
416 Ibid, 2007:409.

# PSALM 120

*Levavi oculos meos in montes: Ja.*

*If you don't want to be seen by anybody, take some dust from under your feet and read this Psalm over it until* **Dominus custodiat** *and throw a part of this dust onto your head and the other part into the face of the person and you will not be seen at all.*

## COMMENTARY:

The Latin in the title is the first half of verse one, *"I have lifted up my eyes to the mountains"*. As mentioned for Psalm 59, Ja may be a contraction of Yah.

Being unseen here seems more likely to be the result of the other person having dust in their eyes!

A Syriac charm (fifth-eighth century CE) for the protection of young children uses this Psalm in its entirety, with the interesting insertion of the following line between verses one and two of the Psalm:

*"That is, I expect a guardian angel from every hill at every hour against weakness"*.[417]

This Psalm recited seven times enables one to be able to travel safely alone by night, according to *Sepher Shimmush Tehillim.*[418]

In the *Goetia*, three Shemhamphorash angels are associated with verses of this Psalm. They are the twenty-

---

417 A Syriac Charm, Hazard, 1893:290.
418 The Sixth and Seventh Books of Moses, Peterson, 2008:208.

second angel Yeiael, with verse five, *"The Lord is thy keeper, the Lord is thy protection upon thy right hand"*;[419] the twenty-third angel Melahel, with verse eight *"May the Lord keep thy going in and thy going out; from henceforth now and forever"*;[420] and the forty-second angel Mikael, with verse seven, *"The Lord keepeth thee from all evil: may the Lord keep thy soul"*.[421]

419 The Goetia of Dr Rudd, Skinner & Rankine, 2007:409.
420 Ibid, 2007:409.
421 Ibid, 2007:410.

# PSALM 121

*Lætatus sum in his quæ dicta sunt mihi:*

*Read this Psalm until **Quia illic sederunt sedes in judicio** and you will overcome your enemy.*

## COMMENTARY:

The Latin in the title is the first half of verse one, *"I rejoiced at the things that were said to me"*.

*Sepher Shimmush Tehillim* advises reciting this Psalm thirteen times to be received graciously and with favour when about to address a man of high ranking. It also suggests praying this Psalm when in church to receive a blessing.[422]

---

422 The Sixth and Seventh Books of Moses, Peterson, 2008:208.

# PSALM 122

**Ad te levavi oculos meos: Raphael.**

*Read this Psalm seven times and God will let you overcome those, [218] who wish to cause some violence against you.*

## COMMENTARY:

The Latin in the title is the first half of verse one, *"To thee have I lifted up my eyes"*. Raphael is the Mercurial archangel, sometimes associated with the Sun.

*Sepher Shimmush Tehillim* suggests writing this Psalm with the name of a servant on a lead or tin plate to compel the servant to return.[423]

---

423 The Sixth and Seventh Books of Moses, Peterson, 2008:208.

# PSALM 123

*Nisi quia Dominus erat in nobis.*

*Read this Psalm seven times and you will find your path and if you read it over a cup of spring or well water, which has never seen the sun and if you sprinkle this Psalm with it, you will be lucky if you bury it in your house.*

**COMMENTARY:**

The Latin in the title is most of verse one, *"If it had not been that the Lord was with us"*.

The second half of verse three and first half of verse four, *"When their fury was enkindled against us, perhaps the waters had swallowed us up"*, is used in the experiment to bring enmity between two friends in *Munich CLM 849.*[424]

This is a water protection Psalm in *Sepher Shimmush Tehillim*. It may be recited to cross a swollen stream safely and also for journeys on water, when it should be recited before entering the ship.[425]

---

424 Forbidden Rites, Kieckhefer, 1997:72.
425 The Sixth and Seventh Books of Moses, Peterson, 2008:208.

# PSALM 124

*Qui confidunt in Domino sicut mons Sion: Adonay:*

*Write this Psalm and attach it to a sick man and he will have relief immediately and if you bury it in front of your door, you will be fortunate.*

## COMMENTARY:

The Latin in the title is the first half of verse one, *"They that trust in the Lord shall be as Mount Sion"*. Adonay (ADNI), meaning *'Lord'* is the divine name substituted for Tetragrammaton (IHVH) in Judaism, which has become one of the main divine names in the grimoires and the Qabalah.

The use in *Sepher Shimmush Tehillim* is for safe passage in a country, where one has avowed enemies. Take salt in both hands and pronounce the Psalm over it seven times and scatter it into the air towards the Four Quarters of the Globe.[426]

Verse 1, *"They that trust in the Lord shall be as mount Sion: he shall not be moved for ever that dwelleth"*, is used around the edge of a Jupiterian Pentacle used for causing spirits to come and obey (see Jupiter 3, Appendix 4). This verse is also used on a derivative Solar Pentacle against fear and terror of the night (see Sun 4, Appendix 5).

---

426 The Sixth and Seventh Books of Moses, Peterson, 2008:208.

# PSALM 125

*In convertendo Dominus captivitatem Sion, Eloym*

*Read this Psalm seven times over seeds and sow them straight away and the God's blessing will be upon the seeds and upon the field.*

## COMMENTARY:

The Latin in the title is the first half of verse one, *"When the Lord brought back the captivity of Sion"*. Eloym is a form of the divine name Elohim (*'Gods'*) which is used throughout the grimoires, and particularly in the *Book of Genesis*.

*Sepher Shimmush Tehillim* recommends this Psalm, with the names of the anti-Lilith angels, Samoy, Sansenoy and Semangelof, be written on charms and placed in the four corners of a house to protect children through infancy. [427]

This Psalm is one of those in the sequence of nineteen (130, 14, 101, 8, 83, 67, 71, 132, 112, 125, 45, 46, 21, 50, 129, 138, 48, 109, 52) recited for conjuration of the wax used in making the Pentacles in the *Key of Solomon*.[428]

---

427 The Sixth and Seventh Books of Moses, Peterson, 2008:208.
428 The Key of Solomon the King, Mathers, 1976:114.

# PSALM 126

## *Nisi Dominus adificaverit domum. Ja*

*Write this Psalm with some saffron and rosewater and perfume it with wood of aloe and also write these characters and bind them to the thigh of the enchanted husband. Then read this Psalm seven times over a glass of wine and give it to the husband to drink [219] and the charm will be destroyed immediately.*

*The Moon in ♐ hour of ♃*

## PRAYER

*Oh God, Sovereign Architect of Houses, we pray to Thee to protect us and to fulfil our desires so that Thou mayest promise that we may be united with your Chosen through Our Lord Jesus Christ. So mote it be.*

## COMMENTARY:

The Latin in the title is the opening words of verse one, *"Unless the Lord build the house"*. As mentioned for Psalm 59, Ja may be a contraction of Yah.

Again the implication is that an ink is made with the saffron and rosewater.

*Sepher Shimmush Tehillim* suggests this Psalm written on a charm and worn around a boy's neck from the moment of birth to guard him through life. [429]

429 The Sixth and Seventh Books of Moses, Peterson, 2008:209.

# PSALM 127

*Beati omnes qui timent Dominum.*

*Write this Psalm until* **Uxor tua sicut vitis abundeus in lateribus Domus tuæ** *and bury it at the root of a vine and the vineyard will bear fruit; it is also good for sight.*
*The Moon as above this one.*

## COMMENTARY:

The Latin in the title is the first half of verse one, *"Blessed are all they that fear the Lord"*.

The theme of fruitfulness is also seen in a medieval Judeo-Arabic text on the magical use of the Psalms, which recommended the use of the Psalm written on kosher parchment to be carried at all times for preventing miscarriage and being successfully fruitful.[430]

This Psalm is advocated by *Sepher Shimmush Tehillim* to protect a pregnant mother and child from harm during childbirth when written on pure parchment and hung upon her.[431]

---

430 A Time to Be Born: Customs and Folklore of Jewish Birth, Klein, 2000:111.
431 The Sixth and Seventh Books of Moses, Peterson, 2008:209.

# PSALM 128

*Sæpe expugnaverunt me a juvente mea:*

*Write this Psalm on a blade of glass then wash it with water and sprinkle it in the house where will be are lamiæ[432] and lemuræ[433] they will no longer appear. The Moon as above.*

## COMMENTARY:

The Latin in the title is most of verse one, *"Often have they fought against me from my youth"*.

*Sepher Shimmush Tehillim* states this Psalm enables the individual to be able to live piously and virtuously, when prayed daily after morning prayers.[434]

432 Lamia is a monster from Greek mythology – a vampiric half-woman, half serpent demon who preyed on young men.
433 Lemures were vengeful and malignant ghosts in Roman mythology.
434 The Sixth and Seventh Books of Moses, Peterson, 2008:209.

# PSALM 129

## *De profundis clamavi ad te Domine*

*Write this Psalm along with Psalm **CIX** on four cards
and bury them at the four corners of a field or a house.
Blessings will be upon them. The Moon as above.*
*[220]*

## COMMENTARY:

The Latin in the title is verse one, *"Out of the depths I
have cried to thee, O Lord"*. Psalm 109 (CIX) by itself does not
have such a use, so this is a combination use.

This is the sixth of the seven Penitential Psalms.

According to *Sepher Shimmush Tehillim* praying this
Psalm to the four quarters of the Earth will enable a person
to leave a besieged city in safety without being noticed by the
sentries, as a heavy sleep will overcome them.[435]

This Psalm is one of those in the sequence of nineteen
(130, 14, 101, 8, 83, 67, 71, 132, 112, 125, 45, 46, 21, 50,
129, 138, 48, 109, 52) recited for conjuration of the wax
used in making the Pentacles in the *Key of Solomon*.[436]

This is the last Psalm in the sequence of seven (3, 8, 30,
41, 59, 50, 129) for use in the preparation of the needle,
burin and other iron instruments in the *Key of Solomon*.[437]

---

435 The Sixth and Seventh Books of Moses, Peterson, 2008:209.
436 The Key of Solomon the King, Mathers, 1976:114.
437 Ibid, 1976:115.

# PSALM 130

## *Domine non est exaltatum cor meum: Adonay Sabaoth:*

*Write this Psalm and attach it to your right arm and you will not have any bad dreams.*

## COMMENTARY:

The Latin in the title is the opening words of verse one, *"Lord, my heart is not exalted"*. Adonay (ADNI), meaning *'Lord'* is the divine name substituted for Tetragrammaton (IHVH) in Judaism, which has become one of the main divine names in the grimoires and the Qabalah. Sabaoth, meaning *'Hosts'*, is seen in divine names such as Jahveh Sabaoth, *'God of Hosts'*.

*Sepher Shimmush Tehillim* recommends this Psalm for one who needs to moderate extreme pride, by reciting it three times daily after the morning and evening prayers.[438]

This Psalm is one of those in the sequence of nineteen (130, 14, 101, 8, 83, 67, 71, 132, 112, 125, 45, 46, 21, 50, 129, 138, 48, 109, 52) recited for conjuration of the wax used in making the Pentacles in the *Key of Solomon*.[439]

In the *Goetia*, the thirty-fourth Shemhamphorash angel, Lehachiah, is associated with verse three of this Psalm, *"Let Israel hope in the Lord, from henceforth now and forever"*.[440]

---

438 The Sixth and Seventh Books of Moses, Peterson, 2008:209.
439 The Key of Solomon the King, Mathers, 1976:114.
440 The Goetia of Dr Rudd, 2007:410.

# PSALM 131

## *Memento Domine David*

*Write this Psalm until **Viduam ejus benediciens benediciam** and attach it to any fishing nets and you will catch a lot of fish, of which some will have these characters.*

## COMMENTARY:

The Latin in the title is the first half of verse one, *"O Lord, remember David"*.

*Sepher Shimmush Tehillim* gives this as a Psalm of repentance, to be repeated daily by one who has perjured an oath and not performed a sworn obligation, and does not wish to repeat a similar crime in the future.[441]

---

441 The Sixth and Seventh Books of Moses, Peterson, 2008:209.

# PSALM 132

## *Ecce quam bonum & quam jucundum*

*Write this Psalm and read it seven times over some good rose oil and rub your face with it and you will be welcomed everywhere.*

## COMMENTARY:

The Latin in the title is the first half of verse one, *"Behold how good and how pleasant it is"*.

This Psalm is recommended by *Sepher Shimmush Tehillim* to retain love and gain more friends, possibly being the source of *Le Livre d'Or* usage.[442]

This Psalm is one of those in the sequence of nineteen (130, 14, 101, 8, 83, 67, 71, 132, 112, 125, 45, 46, 21, 50, 129, 138, 48, 109, 52) recited for conjuration of the wax used in making the Pentacles in the *Key of Solomon*.[443]

---

442 The Sixth and Seventh Books of Moses, Peterson, 2008:210.
443 The Key of Solomon the King, Mathers, 1976:114.

# PSALM 133

## *Ecce nunc benedicite Dominum,*

*Read this Psalm seven times in the morning and also at night and your goods will increase.*

**COMMENTARY:**

The Latin in the title is the opening words of verse one, *"Behold now bless ye the Lord"*.

*Sepher Shimmush Tehillim* declares that every person should repeat this Psalm before entering a college.[444]

This is the last of the three Psalms (71, 116, 133) used in the conjuration of the parchment in the *Key of Solomon.*[445] It is also the third of the four (81, 71, 133, 63) to be spoken over the silken cloth as part of its consecration, prior to its use for wrapping the instruments of the Art in the *Key of Solomon.*[446]

---

444 The Sixth and Seventh Books of Moses, Peterson, 2008:210.
445 The Key of Solomon the King, Mathers, 1976:113.
446 The Key of Solomon the King, Mathers, 1976:116.

# PSALM 134

## *Laudate nomen Domini, Elot.*

*If you are sick, read this Psalm seven times over some good oil and rub your face with it and you will be healed.*

*Put some tuff[447] stone into some wine at night time and wash the eyes of a sick person while reading this Psalm and he will be healed.*

*[221]*

## COMMENTARY:

The Latin in the title is the first half of verse one, *"Praise ye the name of the Lord"*.

*Sepher Shimmush Tehillim* recommends reciting this Psalm daily after morning and evening prayers for the repenting of sins and consecrating one's life to the service of God.[448]

This Psalm is the last in the sequence of eight Psalms (8, 21, 27, 29, 32, 51, 72, 134) to be recited during the consecration of the Pentacles in the *Key of Solomon*. The Pentacle is held over the incense towards the rising sun and the Psalms recited with devotion.[449]

Part of verse 16, *"they have eyes, but they see not"*, is one of the two verses used around a Solar Pentacle for operations of invisibility (see Sun 6, Appendix 4).

---

447 A kind of volcanic stone.
448 The Sixth and Seventh Books of Moses, Peterson, 2008:210.
449 The Veritable Key of Solomon, Skinner & Rankine, 2008:304.

# PSALM 135

## Confitemini Domino quoniam bonus

*Read this Psalm in front of the door of your enemy until*
**Liberavit eos** *and you will overcome him.*

**COMMENTARY:**

The Latin in the title is the first half of verse one, *"Praise the Lord, for he is good"*.

*Sepher Shimmush Tehillim* advises praying this Psalm before making confession for the penitent who wishes for a renewal of spirit after confession of transgressions, sins and misdeeds.[450]

---

450 The Sixth and Seventh Books of Moses, Peterson, 2008:210.

# PSALM 136

*Super flumina Babylonis, illic sedimus & flevinus.*

*Write this Psalm with a woman's menstrual blood, along with the names of her husband and her mother until **ad fundamentum in ea** and perfume it with myrrh and place it in a phial sealed well with wax and bury it in water flowing towards the East. Then read this Psalm seven times over it in the name of the woman and her husband. The loss of blood will cease and the blood will flow no longer. The Moon as before this one.*

## COMMENTARY:

The Latin in the title is most of verse one, *"Upon the rivers of Babylon, there we sat and wept"*.

*Sepher Shimmush Tehillim* states that this Psalm is said to root inveterate hate, envy and malice out of the heart.[451]

---

451 The Sixth and Seventh Books of Moses, Peterson, 2008:210.

# PSALM 137

## *Confitebor tibi Domine in toto corde meo*

*Read this Psalm seven times over rose water and rub your face with it and write it out and attach it to your arm and you will be delivered from prison. The Moon as before this one.*

**COMMENTARY:**

The Latin in the title is the opening words of verse one, *"I will praise thee, O Lord, with my whole heart"*.

*Sepher Shimmush Tehillim* suggests this Psalm to produce love and friendship.[452]

---

452 The Sixth and Seventh Books of Moses, Peterson, 2008:210.

# PSALM 138

*Domine probasti me & cognovisti me:*

*Read this Psalm seven times every day and God will make you contrite with true penitence from your bawdiness and from adultery and you will be saved.*
*[222]*

## COMMENTARY:

The Latin in the title is verse one, *"Lord, thou hast proved me, and known me"*.

*Sepher Shimmush Tehillim* advises this Psalm to preserve and increase love among married people.[453]

This Psalm is one of those in the sequence of nineteen (130, 14, 101, 8, 83, 67, 71, 132, 112, 125, 45, 46, 21, 50, 129, 138, 48, 109, 52) recited for conjuration of the wax used in making the Pentacles in the *Key of Solomon*.[454]

---

453 The Sixth and Seventh Books of Moses, Peterson, 2008:210.
454 The Key of Solomon the King, Mathers, 1976:114.

# PSALM 139

*Eripe me Domine ab homine malo. Heloe.*

*Read this Psalm for seven days, seven times in the evening and seven times in morning until **Venenum aspidum sub labiis eorum** and be chaste during these seven days. Whoever has taken poison will be saved if he does so.*

## COMMENTARY:

The Latin in the title is the first half of verse two, *"Deliver me, O Lord, from the evil man"* Heloe is found as a divine name in the *Lemegeton*.

*Sepher Shimmush Tehillim* gives this Psalm to remove growing hatred between a man and his wife.[455]

In the *Goetia*, the twenty-seventh Shemhamphorash angel, Yerathel, is associated with verse two of this Psalm, *"Deliver me, O Lord, from the evil man: rescue me from the unjust man"*.[456]

---

455 The Sixth and Seventh Books of Moses, Peterson, 2008:210.
456 The Goetia of Dr Rudd, Skinner, & Rankine, 2009:409.

# PSALM 140

*Domine clamavi ad te exaudi me. Elion.*

*When you meet scoundrels, recite this Psalm seven times and you will be delivered from them through the aid of God.*

## COMMENTARY:

The Latin in the title is the first half of verse one, *"I have cried to thee, O Lord, hear me"*. Elion, meaning *'Highest God'*, is a divine name sometimes used for the Sephira of Kether in Qabalah, and was originally the name of a Canaanite god.

*Sepher Shimmush Tehillim* suggests this Psalm to relieve a sense of oppression.[457]

---

457 The Sixth and Seventh Books of Moses, Peterson, 2008:210.

# PSALM 141

## *Voce mea ad Dominum clamavi*

*Read this Psalm seven times in the morning as well as in the evening until **Educ de custodia animam meam** and by means of the Grace of God, you will leave prison. Also write this Psalm along with its characters and hang them in the air; the servant who has taken flight will return to you.*

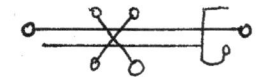 

## COMMENTARY:

The Latin in the title is the first half of verse two, *"I cried to the Lord with my voice"*.

*Sepher Shimmush Tehillim* recommends this Psalm to cure pain in the thighs.[458]

This Psalm is the third of three written with some characters on a piece of virgin parchment and placed under the pillow for a dream vision of a thief and where he placed stolen goods.[459]

---

458 The Sixth and Seventh Books of Moses, Peterson, 2008:210.
459 A Collection of Magical Secrets, Skinner, Rankine & Barron, 2009:23.

# PSALM 142

*Domine exaudi orationem meam. Jad.*

*Write this Psalm and read it until* **Eripe me de inimicis meis Domine** *and you will be delivered from prison; it has the same effect if you are in any kind of difficulty.*
*[223]*

**COMMENTARY:**

The Latin in the title is the opening words of verse one, *"Hear, O Lord, my prayer"*. Jad may be a corruption of the Hebrew letter Yod, which like Aleph is often used as a shorthand for the divine.

This is the last of the seven Penitential Psalms.

*Sepher Shimmush Tehillim* gives this Psalm for removing sharp pains in the arms.[460]

---

460 The Sixth and Seventh Books of Moses, Peterson, 2008:210.

# PSALM 143

## *Benedictus Dominus Deus meus,*

*Read this Psalm seven times and write the characters that follow and carry it upon you and you will be victorious in combats.*

*It is also good for a woman in labour, if it is written on her hip and here is where it should be attached.*

*If anyone is in a shipwreck, read it until **& libera me de aquis multis** and he will be saved*

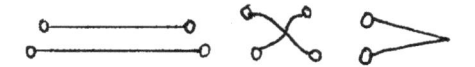

*The Moon as before this one.*

## COMMENTARY:

The Latin in the title is the opening words of verse one, *"Blessed be the Lord my God"*.

*Sepher Shimmush Tehillim* suggests this Psalm to repair a broken arm, when prayed over it.[461]

---

461 The Sixth and Seventh Books of Moses, Peterson, 2008:210.

# PSALM 144

*Exaltabo te Deus meus Rex; Sala.*

*Read this Psalm seven times over oil and rub a woman's body with it and her husband will return to her then write it down and bury it in front of the door.*
*If you read this Psalm seven times and if you rub sick man's face with this oil, he will be healed also. The Moon as above.*

## COMMENTARY:

The Latin in the title is the opening words of verse one, *"I will extol thee, O God my king"*.

In the eleventh century Hekhalot text *Tefillat Hamnuna Sava* (*The Prayer by Hamnuna the Elder*), this Psalm is repeated thrice as the corpus of the Ashre prayer by the mystic in his preparation, as part of the instructions given by the archangel Sagnasgiel (Metatron). The Ashre prayer is Psalm 143:15 followed by the whole of Psalm 144 followed by Psalm 83:5.[462]

*Sepher Shimmush Tehillim* recommends this Psalm to drive away ghosts and apparitions instantly, when prayed in conjunction with Psalm 143.[463]

In the *Goetia*, four Shemhamphorash angels are associated with verses of this Psalm. These are the forty-ninth angel Vehuel, with verse three, *"Great is the Lord, and*

---

462 Jewish Mysticism in the Geonic Period, Herrmann, 2005:184.
463 The Sixth and Seventh Books of Moses, Peterson, 2008:210.

*greatly to be praised: and of his greatness there is no end"*;[464] the fiftieth angel Daniel, with verse eight *"The Lord is gracious and merciful: patient and plenteous in mercy"*;[465] the fifty-sixth angel Poiel, with verse fourteen *"The Lord lifteth up all that fall: and setteth up all that are cast down"*;[466] and the sixtieth angel Mitzrael, with verse seventeen, *"The Lord is just in all his ways: and holy in all his works"*.[467]

A Jewish tradition states that whoever recites this Psalm three times a day is assured of a place in the world to come (*b Ber 4b*).[468]

464 The Goetia of Dr Rudd, Skinner & Rankine, 2007:411.
465 Ibid, 2007:411.
466 Ibid, 2007:411.
467 Ibid, 2007:411.
468 Jewish Mysticism in the Geonic Period, Herrmann, 2005:187.

# PSALM 145

## *Lauda anima mea Dominum*

*Read this Psalm seven times over oil and rub a sick man with it while reciting it and he will be healed.*
*If you read it until **Dominus erigit adlisos: Dominus diligit justos** and rub broken bones with this oil, they will knit back together.*
*[224]*

**COMMENTARY:**

The Latin in the title is the opening words of verse two, *"Praise the Lord, O my soul"*.

A version of the conjuration of the Prince of the Thumb using a variant of verse six of this Psalm is found in *Munich CLM 849*, for obtaining information about a theft by gazing into a fingernail.[469] The phrase is spoken whilst drawing the third of the three protective circles with the sword.[470]

*Sepher Shimmush Tehillim* recommends this Psalm for healing from a dangerous sword wound that needs surgical assistance. The healing of serious wounds suggests this use may have influenced that in *Le Livre d'Or*.[471]

---

469 Forbidden Rites, Kieckhefer, 1997:329.
470 For more on the Princes of the Thumb see A Collection of Magical Secrets, Skinner, Rankine & Barron, 2009.
471 The Sixth and Seventh Books of Moses, Peterson, 2008:210.

# PSALM 146

*Laudate Dominum quoniam bonus est psalmus.*
**Sach**

*Read out this Psalm seven times over oil until **& alligat contritiones eorum** and rub a sick man with is and he will be healed.*
*If you wish to share anything with anyone, read this Psalm and your shared portion will be good.*

## COMMENTARY:

The Latin in the title is the first half of verse one, *"Praise ye the Lord, because psalm is good"*.

In the *Sepher Shimmush Tehillim*, this Psalm is also used for healing, though in that instance it is for a man seriously wounded by a sword or other weapon.[472]

In the *Goetia*, the twenty-fourth Shemhamphorash angel, Chahuiah, is associated with verse eleven of this Psalm, *"The Lord taketh pleasure in them that fear him: and in them that hope in his mercy"*.[473]

---

472 The Sixth and Seventh Books of Moses, Peterson, 2008:210.
473 The Goetia of Dr Rudd, Skinner & Rankine, 2007:409.

# PSALM 147

## *Lauda Jerusalem Dominum*

*Write this Psalm with some saffron mixed with some rose water and perfume it with wood of aloe and bury it at the foundations of a house. When you build upon it, God's Blessings will be present.*

*The Moon in ♐ hour of ♃.*

## COMMENTARY:

The Latin in the title is the first half of verse one, *"Praise the Lord, O Jerusalem"*.

*Sepher Shimmush Tehillim* recommends this Psalm for healing dangerous and deadly wounds, bites and stings of salamanders, lizards, snakes, scorpions and other poisonous creatures.[474]

---

474 The Sixth and Seventh Books of Moses, Peterson, 2008:211.

# PSALM 148

## *Lauda Dominum de Cœlis.*

*If someone reads this Psalm seven times every day in his house, the Dæmon will leave there and the house will be full of blessings. It is also good for a sick woman, when you read it over pure oil and rub her with it. She will be healed.*

## COMMENTARY:

The Latin in the title is the first half of verse one, *"Praise ye the Lord from the heavens"*.

*Sepher Shimmush Tehillim* states that when prayed with absolute trust this Psalm will check an uncontrolled fire.[475]

Verse eight, *"Fire, hail, snow, ice, stormy winds which fulfil his word:"* is written around the edge of a Saturnian Pentacle for protection from hail and storms and the good of the earth (see Saturn 1, Appendix 5).

---

475 The Sixth and Seventh Books of Moses, Peterson, 2008:211.

# PSALM 149

## Cantata Domino canticum novum

*Recite this Psalm seven times over oil and rub a sick woman's body with it and she will heal.*
*[225]*

## COMMENTARY:

The Latin in the title is the first half of verse one, *"Sing ye to the Lord a new canticle"*.

*Sepher Shimmush Tehillim* states that like the previous Psalm, when prayed with absolute trust this Psalm will check an uncontrolled fire.[476]

---

476 The Sixth and Seventh Books of Moses, Peterson, 2008:211.

# PSALM 150

## *Laudate Dominum in sanctis ejus*

*Recite this Psalm seven times over wheat and over oil and they will be multiplied to you with the aid of God. Take note that after every Psalm it is necessary to read a little prayer to God and do all things when the Moon is Waxing and under the Sign and during the Hour that is indicated. It would be better, however, if the Signs were in their ascendancy at the same time as the Waxing Moon.*

*When thunder and lightning are heard, take the Symbol of St Athanasius in your hand and read it until **Without the three persons being confused** and immediately they will be dispersed and if you read it over a sick person with three Pater's[477] and three Ave's,[478] he will be delivered and healed through the Virtue of God.*

## COMMENTARY:

The Latin in the title is the first half of verse one, *"Praise ye the Lord in his holy places"*.

*Sepher Shimmush Tehillim* declares that this psalm should be repeated by every fortunate person, who has

---

477 "Our Father's".
478 "Hail Mary's".

escaped danger and give praise to the Lord of Hosts with thanks in his heart.[479]

---

479 The Sixth and Seventh Books of Moses, Peterson, 2008:211.

# THE SYMBOL OF ST ATHANASIUS OR THE ATHANASIAN CREED

*I*

*Whosoever wishes to be saved, before all things it is necessary that he knows and holds the Catholic Faith.*

*II*

*And if anyone does not conserve it undefiled and without doubt, he will perish eternally.*

*[226]*

*III*

*Thus, the Catholic Faith consists in adoring one Sole God in three Persons in one Sole Godhead.*

*IV*

*Without the three Persons being confused and without separating the Substance*

*V*

*For there is one Person of The Father, another of The Son and another of The Holy Ghost.*

*VI*

*But the Godhead of The Father, The Son and Holy Ghost
is one and the same, Their glory is equal and Their
majesty co-eternal.*

*VII*

*Such as The Father is, such is The Son, such is The Holy
Ghost.*

*VIII*

*The Father is Uncreate, The Son is Uncreate and The
Holy Ghost is Uncreate.*

*IX*

*The Father is Great,[480] The Son is Great, The Holy Ghost
is Great.*

*X*

*The Father is Eternal, The Son is Eternal, The Holy
Ghost is Eternal.*

*XI*

*And yet they are not Three Eternal Beings, but One
Eternal Being.*

*[227]*

---

480 Other translations render this as "Incomprehensible"

## XII

*As also they are not Three Uncreated Beings, nor Three Great[481] Beings, but One Uncreated Being and One Great Being.*

## XIII

*In the same way, The Father is Almighty, The Son is Almighty and The Holy Ghost is Almighty.*

## XIV

*And yet, they are not Three Almighty Beings, but One Almighty Being.*

## XV

*Thus is The Father God, The Son is God, The Holy Ghost is God.*

## XVI

*And likewise, They are not Three Gods, but One Sole God.*

## XVII

*Thus is The Father Lord, The Son is Lord and The Holy Ghost is Lord.*

## XVIII

*And yet, They are not Three Lords, but One Sole Lord.*

---

481 Or incomprehensible – as above

## XIX

*For as the Truth commands us to confess that each Person is God and Lord, so does the Catholic Religion prohibit us from calling Them Three Gods or Three Lords.*

## XX

*The Father knows no beginning, nor has he been made, nor has he been begotten.*

*[228]*

## XXI

*The Son has been neither made, nor created but was begotten of the Sole Father.*

## XXII

*The Holy Ghost has been neither made nor created nor begotten but proceeds from the Father and the Son.*

## XXIII

*There is therefore but One Sole Father, not Three Fathers, One Sole Son, not Three Sons, One Sole Holy Ghost, not Three Holy Ghosts.*

## XXIV

*And in this Trinity No One comes First or Last, No One is greater or lesser, but each of the Three Persons is co-eternal and equal together.*

## XXV

*So that in all things and in all places as has been said beforehand, the Unity in Trinity and the Trinity in Unity is to be worshipped.*

## XXVI

*Whosoever wishes, therefore, to be saved must hold these sentiments of the Trinity.*

## XXVII

*But for Eternal Salvation, it is necessary that each person firmly believe in the incarnation of Our Lord Jesus Christ.*

## XXVIII

*This is therefore pure and true faith that obliges us to believe and to [229] confess that Our Lord Jesus Christ the Son of God, is God and Man.*

## XXIX

*God was begotten of the Substance of the Father before all the Ages and Man was born of the Substance of His Mother into the World.[482]*

## XXX

*Perfect God, Perfect Man composed of a rational soul and human flesh.*

---

482 Or Time

## XXXI

*Equal to The Father according to his Godhead and inferior to The Father according to his Humanity.*

## XXXII

*Yet although He is God and Man, He is not two Christs, but One Sole Jesus Christ.*

## XXXIII

*I say One, not by the transformation of Godhead into Humanity, but by the union of the nature of Mankind to the nature of God.*

## XXXIV

*One, not through the confusion of Substance but by Unity of Person.*

## XXXV

*For as the rational soul is One Sole Man of flesh, thus God is one Sole Jesus Christ with Man.*

*[230]*

## XXXVI

*He, who has suffered death for our Salvation, descended into Hell and on the third day, He rose from the dead.*

## XXXVII

*He, who ascended into Heaven, is seated at the Right Hand of God The Father Almighty and from whence He will come to judge the quick and the dead.*

*XXXVIII*

*At whose coming all men shall rise again in body and give account for their own actions.*

*XXXIX*

*And they that have done good deeds will go into Life Eternal and they that have done evil will go into eternal fire.*

*XL*

*This is the Catholic Faith and whosoever will not believe in it sincerely and firmly will not be saved.*

*END*

## COMMENTARY:

This is one of the Creeds given place in the Catholic Church, which gives a clear Commentary: of the doctrines of the Trinity and the Incarnation. Most other Creeds deal with other *'fundamental truths'*, whereas this Creed (cf. The Nicene Creed) deals with these two exclusively.

The Creed is thought to have been written by another Archbishop of Alexandria or his provincial synods around the year 361 CE, rather than by St Athanasius (who was Pope of Alexandria), to whom it is credited. However, there is significant controversy and debate surrounding its author and date of origin.

Like the Psalms, the Creed was also used for magical

purposes. The opening words of the Athanasian Creed are spoken three times over a pregnant woman's body in the fifteenth century *Sloane MS 962* to ease childbirth, interestingly followed by the words of the Sator magic square.

The Athanasian Creed is also to be found in *Verus Jesuitarum Libellus* (*The True Petition of the Jesuits*). In that small grimoire which is believed to date to the nineteenth century it is recited along with Psalm 129 at the end of the Discharge of the Spirit from the first conjuration in the manuscript.

# APPENDICES

# 1. Précis of all of Uses of the Psalms in Le Livre d'Or

| Psalm | Purpose | Repetition | Ingredients | Equipment | Notes |
|---|---|---|---|---|---|
| 1 | Pregnancy protection | | Mastic | Written on paper | Bound to right arm |
| 2 | Curing over-eating pains | | Oil | | Anointed with oil |
| 2 | Welcome by a prince | | Oil | Tablet | Ash tablet and anoint self with oil |
| 3 | Headache cure | | | Written on paper | Bound round head |
| 4 | Protection from watery peril and accidents | | | | |
| 4 | Friendship of great people | Seven | | | Characters written on left hand |

| | | | | | |
|---|---|---|---|---|---|
| 5 | Protection from malicious people | Three | Olive oil | | Head anointed and characters written on hand |
| 5 | Friendships of lords | Three | Olive oil | | Head anointed and characters written on hand |
| 6 | Dealing with Judges | Seven | | | |
| 6 | Curing eye disease | Seven | | | Repeated for three days |
| 7 | Protection from enemies | | Earth | | Recite over earth and throw in direction of enemies |
| 7 | Vanquishing enemies | Four | Water | Earthenware jar | Water thrown where enemies pass |
| 8 | Prevent children crying | | | Written on paper | Bound on right arm |
| 8 | Holding and moving honey bees | | | | Recite first verse only |

| No. | Purpose | | Ingredient | Vessel | Method |
|---|---|---|---|---|---|
| 9 | Honoured by king or prince | | Olive oil | Glass plate | Write on plate, wash with oil and anoint face with oil |
| 10 | Killing enemies | | | Parchment | Buried under dead person's head |
| 11 | Preventing slander by enemies | | Borax, water | Glass plate | Read Psalm over water, bury plate under enemy's door |
| 12 | Protection from rogues | Three | | | |
| 12 | Making a child amenable to education | | Holy water | Drinking glass | Write characters, wash with holy water and give to child to drink |
| 13 | Appearing majestic | | Mastic, musk, pure water | | Write characters, perfume and wash then pour water on doorstep |
| 14 | Approaching a prince | | | | Carry characters on you |
| 15 | Protection from enchantment | | | | Carry characters on you |

| 16 | Avoiding scandal | Seven | Mastic | | Perfume characters and carry on you |
| 17 | Healing sick people | | Pure water | Earthenware bowl | Recite over bowl of water and place in room. |
| 18 | Assisting pregnancy | | Holy water, aloes | Written on paper, glass plate | Write on paper and place under feet, after birth written on plate, perfumed with aloes, washed with water and given to her to drink and rubbed on stomach |
| 19 | Healing sick person | | | | |
| 20 | Being well received and honoured | Seven | Rose oil, mastic | Written on tablet | Perfume tablet, wash with oil then use to anoint face |
| 21 | Protection from petty & malicious people | Seven | | | |
| 21 | Vanquishing enemy | | Mastic, pure water | Glass plate | Write characters on plate, perfume then wash & bury under enemy's doorway |
| 22 | Protection when travelling | | Oil | | Read Psalm over oil and anoint face with it |

| Psalm | Purpose | Ingredients | Method | Additional instruction |
|---|---|---|---|---|
| 23 | To be loved | Musk, saffron, rose water | | Write characters and perfume with the fragrances |
| 24 | Helping a sick person sleep | | Written on paper | Place Psalm under head |
| 25 | Destroying enchantments | | | |
| 25 | Protection from enemies | | | |
| 26 | Protecting vine tree | Spring water | Write Psalm and wash in spring water used to water tree | |
| 26 | Curing worms for a child | | Use Saint name possessed by child | |
| 27 | Protection from your children and close friends | | | |
| 27 | Reconciliation with enemies | Three | | Form character with fingers |

| Psalm | Purpose | Number | Ingredient | Writing | Instructions |
| --- | --- | --- | --- | --- | --- |
| 28 | Healing sick man | | Barley beer | | Recite Psalm in his ear whilst drinking beer |
| 28 | House blessing | | Nutmeg | Write on paper | Perfume with nutmeg and bury at four corners of house |
| 29 | Curing sickness | Seven & Seven | Pure water, good oil | | Recite Psalm seven times over water then bathe, seven times over oil and anoint |
| 30 | Release from prison | Two & Two | Bread | | Write characters on bread and eat, recite Psalm twice by day and by night |
| 31 | Removing desire | Seven | Holy Water, Mastic | Write characters on paper | Recite Psalm seven times over holy water and wash, perfume characters and bind to right arm |
| 32 | To ensure conception | | Mastic, incense | Write characters on paper | Perfume with mastic & incense & bind on her right arm |
| 33 | Heal toothache or fractured bone | Seven | Date stones | | Go to crossroads, recite Psalm 7 times, burn date stones and smoke face |
| 34 | Access to a Prince | Seven | | Write Psalm on paper | Bind on right arm |

| Psalm | Purpose | Number | Ingredients | Write | Instructions |
|---|---|---|---|---|---|
| 35 | Safe pregnancy | | | Write Psalm on paper | Place paper in hood or bind to right arm |
| 36 | Destroying your enemy and his family | | | Write Psalm on paper | Bury paper under front door |
| 37 | Healing eye pain | | Holy water, mastic, incense | Write characters on paper | Read Psalm over holy water at Christmas & wash eyes, perfume characters with mastic & incense and hang round neck |
| 38 | Removing bad dreams | | | | Write Psalm on right side of face |
| 39 | Preventing miscarriage | | | Write characters and Psalm on paper | Bind paper on right arm |
| 40 | Controlling an untrusted mistress | Seven | Rose oil, saffron, rose water | Goat vellum | Read Psalm 7 times over oil and anoint face |
| 41 | Dispersing enemies | | | | Recited at Vespers |
| 42 | Access to a king or prince | | | Write Psalm on paper | Bind paper on right arm |

| Psalm | Purpose | | Ingredient | Method | Use |
|---|---|---|---|---|---|
| 43 | Destroying a enemy | | Bird's blood | Write Psalm on paper in blood | Bury paper under enemy's front door |
| 44 | Gaining a desired person | | Myrrh, aromatic gum, cinnamon | Write Psalm and name on paper | Perfume paper and bury it on front of door |
| 45 | For armed combat | Seven | | | |
| 46 | Lucky in affairs | Seven | | Write Psalm on paper | Carry paper and read 7 times a day |
| 47 | Seeing a thief | | | Write Psalm and characters on paper | Place paper above head of bed |
| 48 | To be loved and cherished | | | Write Psalm on paper | Carry paper |
| 49 | Killing and distributing a sheep to the poor | Seven | | | Read Psalm 7 times |
| 50 | Protection for haemophilia | | | | Write Psalm on person |

| 51 | 52 | 53 | 54 | 55 | 56 | 57 | 58 |
|---|---|---|---|---|---|---|---|
| Pregnancy protection | Vanquishing enemies | Defence against slander to a prince | Preventing an enemy building his house | Stop a pregnant woman bleeding | Protection from beasts in desert | Destroying the effect of an enchantment | Removing sexual enchantment |
| | | Seven | | Seven | Seven | Seven | Seven |
| | Dust | | | Glass of wine | | | |
| Write Psalm on paper | | | Say Psalm over the foundations | Say Psalm 7 times over wine and then give to drink | | | Write Psalm on paper |
| Attach to arm | Read Psalm 7 times over dust and throw in enemies' faces | Read 7 times | | | Recite 7 times | Recite 7 times | Bind to right thigh and recite Psalm 7 times |

| Psalm | Purpose | Number | Ingredient | Method | Instructions |
|---|---|---|---|---|---|
| 59 | Sorting out business affairs and gaining fortune | | Goat blood | Write characters and Psalm on paper | Bury under hinge of door whilst reciting Psalm |
| 60 | Reconciling husband and wife | Three | White cockerels blood | Write characters on paper in blood | Read Psalms 3 times over paper and bind to woman's arm |
| 61 | Killing or vanquishing enemy | Seven | Powder | Altar where Mass is said | Take powder from under altar, read Psalm 7 times over it and scatter in front of enemy's house |
| 62 | Stop a child crying | | | Write Psalm on paper | Attach paper to child's arm |
| 63 | Vanquishing enemies | | | Write characters on paper | Read Psalm over characters and attach paper to arm |
| 64 | Deliverance from need | Seven | | | Recite Psalm 7 times a day |
| 65 | Deliverance from need | Seven & Seven | | | Recite Psalm 7 times in the morning and also evening |
| 66 | Healing sick person | | Pure water | Write characters on paper | Recite Psalm over water and give to drink, attach paper to person |

| Psalm | Purpose | Material | Write | Method |
|---|---|---|---|---|
| 67 | Preventing sleep | | Write Psalm on paper | Bury close to front door |
| 68 | Calming bad weather at sea | | | Read Psalm |
| 69 | Healing a named illness | Incense | Write Psalm on new card | Fumigate 3 or 4 times a day or night and read for 15 days |
| 70 | Winning your case before a judge | | | Say Psalm before approaching judge |
| 71 | Gaining the love of a woman | | Write Psalm on paper with name and mother's name | Attach to your arm |
| 72 | Obtaining your goal or desire | | Write Psalm on paper | Attach to your arm |
| 73 | Causing enemy to flee | Fire | Write Psalm, characters & enemy's name on paper | Burn in fire |
| 74 | Release from prison | | | Recite daily |

| No. | Purpose | Quantity | Liquid | Medium / Vessel | Instructions |
|---|---|---|---|---|---|
| 74 | Increasing merchant's profits | | | Written on fox skin, bound round gold | In Jupiter's hour and day, write Psalm and characters on skin, carried and daily Psalm recitation |
| 75 | Dispelling spirits from a house | | | Write Psalm on paper | Hang from the door on the waxing moon |
| 76 | Dispelling enchantments on a person | | Clean water | Glass plate | Write Psalm on plate, wash with water and give to drink |
| 77 | Vanquishing enemy | Seven | Clean water | Bronze drinking vessel | Write Psalm & characters in vessel, fill with water, recite Psalm 7 times and pour water in front of enemy's door |
| 78 | Being received honourably | Seven | Rose oil | Write characters on a new tablet | Say Psalm 7 times over rose oil, wash tablet with oil and rub it on face |
| 79 | Making a woman chaste | Seven | Clean water | New cooking pot | Write Psalm & characters on pot, fill with water, say Psalm 7 times and wash the woman with the water |
| 80 | To stop haemorrhaging | | Mastic | Write characters on an olive leaf | Perfume leaf, attach to man's arm and then read Psalm |
| 81 | To be honourably received | | Oil or rose oil | Write characters | Read Psalm, wash characters with oil and rub into face |

| Psalm | Purpose | Number | Ingredients | Write on | Method | Instructions |
|---|---|---|---|---|---|---|
| 82 | Destroying your enemy | Seven | Water a woman has washed in | | Cooking pot | Write characters in pot, fill with water a woman has washed in, read Psalm 7 times, pour water in enemy's house |
| 83 | Access to a prince | | | Write on paper | Bind to arm | |
| 84 | Gaining luck | | Laurel leaves, mastic, incense, rose oil | Write on leaves | Perfume leaves, add oil and then anoint face with it | |
| 85 | Blessing wine | Twenty | | | Read Psalm 20 times over wine press, put characters in press | |
| 86 | Fulfilling affairs | | Dove blood, aloe wood, mastic | Write Psalm and characters in blood | Perfume with aloe and mastic and tie to arm | |
| 87 | Vanquishing enemy | | Spring or well water, water a woman has washed in | Write Psalm in new cooking pot, write characters on glass plate | | Put water in pot, wash plate with woman's water and put in pot, then pour the water at enemy's door |
| 88 | Curing headache | | | Write Psalm on person's head | | |
| 88 | House blessing | | Holy water | | | Read Psalm over holy water and sprinkle over house |

| No. | Purpose | Material | Write | Action |
|---|---|---|---|---|
| 89 | Success in ventures | | | Read Psalm |
| 89 | Removing enchantment which separate a man and wife | Once & Once | Write Psalm and characters on piece of linen | Wear linen round neck and recite Psalm morning & night |
| 90 | Protection from enchantment and demons | Dove blood, roses, aloe wood | Write on paper | Write Psalm in blood, perfume with roses and aloe and carry |
| 90 | Protection when travelling by night | Dove blood, roses, aloe wood | Write on paper | Write Psalm in blood, perfume with roses and aloe and carry |
| 90 | Preventing children being frightened | Dove blood, roses, aloe wood | Write on paper | Write Psalm in blood, perfume with roses and aloe and carry |
| 91 | Prevent enemy from harming you | Clean water | Write Psalm on a new plate | Wash plate with water and pour it in enemy's house |
| 92 | Blessing a house | Holy water | Write Psalm on paper | Read Psalm over holy water and bury paper in house |
| 93 | Causing enemies to flee | | | Read Psalm every day |

| Psalm | Purpose | Number | Materials | Write | Method |
|---|---|---|---|---|---|
| 93 | Increasing the profit of a house or mill | | | | Read Psalm every day |
| 94 | Exorcising a demon | | Holy water, holy oil | Write Psalm on a new tablet | Wash tablet with water and oil then anoint sick man with them |
| 95 | Dispelling the traps of rich people | Seven, repeated thrice | | Write enemies' names on paper | Read Psalm 7 times at Vespers for 3 days, and attach paper to arm |
| 96 | Dealing with a hated wife | | Musk, saffron, rosewater, camphor, mastic, aloe | Write Psalm on paper with musk, saffron, rosewater and camphor | Perfume paper with mastic and aloe and bury in front of her door |
| 97 | Preventing a ship sailing | | | | Read Psalm |
| 98 | To be received honourably | Seven | Water | | Read Psalm 7 times over water and wash face with it |
| 99 | Protection from the hate of a mistress | | Raw egg shell, glass of wine | Write Psalm on the egg shell | Place egg shell in wine and give it to her to drink |
| 100 | Protection of a vineyard | | | Write Psalm and characters on paper | Bury at the four corners of the vineyard |

| 100 | 101 | 102 | 103 | 103 | 104 | 105 | 106 |
|---|---|---|---|---|---|---|---|
| Cure an enchanted man | Finding joy and happiness | Curing prolonged sickness | Gaining a woman you desire | Enflaming the heart of any person | Release from prison | To sink a ship | Keeping somebody in prison |
| Seven | | Seven | Seven | Seven | | Seven | |
| Holy water | | Common oil | Bat or black hen blood, new cooking pot, earth of the type used to make pot | Mastic, galbanum, aloe wood, earthenware vessel | | Salt | |
| Write Psalm on a glass plate | | | Write Psalm, characters, your name & woman's name & her parents with gold ink-pen | Write Psalm, characters, woman & her mother's names with bronze or iron ink-pen | Write Psalm on paper | | |
| Wash plate with holy water, recite Psalm 7 times over it and give to the man to drink | Read Psalm before leaving house | Read Psalm over oil 7 times then rub person with it | Place vellum in pot, cover it with earth, place in fire, recite Psalm 7 times while skin burns | Put paper in vessel and seal with wax, place in fire and recite Psalm 7 times | Attach to arm, read Psalm | Read Psalm 7 times over salt and throw on ship | Read Psalm in front of person |

| Psalm | Purpose | Material | Instruction | Application |
|---|---|---|---|---|
| 107 | Approaching a prince or king | Seven | | Read 7 times before approaching |
| 108 | Erasing an enemy | Water women have bathed in | Write Psalm on paper | Wash paper with water and sprinkle water on enemy's house |
| 109 | Initiating childbirth | | Write Psalm on paper | Attach to woman's right thigh |
| 110 | Blessing ground for building on | | | Read Psalm |
| 111 | Causing enemy to perish | Powdered swallow | | Read Psalm over powder for 3 days, then scatter in enemy's house |
| 112 | Increasing profits from house | Holy Water | Read Psalm over holy water & sprinkle house 7 times | |
| 112 | Protection of livestock | | Write Psalm on paper | Put in place where livestock dwells |
| 113 | Stopping fishermen catching fish | Holy water | | Read Psalm over holy water and sprinkle on boats |

| Psalm | Purpose | | Ingredient | Writing | Method |
|---|---|---|---|---|---|
| 114 | Protecting child from sickness & perils | | Mastic, musk, aloe wood | Write Psalm on paper | Perfume paper and attach to right arm of child |
| 115 | Preventing drunkenness, giving healing | Seven | Wine | | Read Psalm 7 times over wine |
| 115 | Approaching a prince or council | | | Write Psalm and characters on paper | Carry on you |
| 116 | Protection from persecution, helping prisoners | | Virgin parchment | Write character and intelligence name on parchment | At sunset recite the Psalm & name of intelligence, & prayer while staring at parchment |
| 117 | Restoring keys to open any room or house | Seven | | | Read Psalm 7 times |
| 118 | Protection from all infirmities | Seven | Mastic | Write Psalm on paper | Read Psalm 7 times, perfume paper with mastic and carry |
| 119 | Causing enemy to flee and perish | Seven | Water a woman has washed in on a Saturday | | Read Psalm 7 times over water and sprinkle on enemy's door |
| 120 | Making yourself unseen | | Dust from under your feet | | Read Psalm over dust, sprinkle some on your head and throw rest in other person's face |

| Psalm | Purpose | | | | Instructions |
|---|---|---|---|---|---|
| 121 | Overcoming enemy | | | | Read Psalm |
| 122 | Overcoming those who wish you violence | Seven | | | Read Psalm 7 times |
| 123 | Finding your path | Seven | | | Read Psalm 7 times |
| 123 | Blessing of house | | Spring or well water | Write Psalm on paper | Read Psalm over cup of water and sprinkle paper, then bury in house |
| 124 | Relief for the sick | | | Write Psalm on paper | Attach to sick person |
| 124 | Gaining fortune | | | Write Psalm on paper | Bury it in front of door |
| 125 | Seed blessing | Seven | | | Read Psalm 7 times over seed and sow immediately |
| 126 | Removing a love enchantment | Seven | Saffron, rosewater, aloe, wine | Write Psalm & characters on paper with saffron & rosewater | Perfume paper with aloe & bind to thigh of man, say Psalm 7 times over glass of wine and make him drink |

| Psalm | Purpose | | Ingredient | Write | Action |
|---|---|---|---|---|---|
| 127 | Encouraging a vineyard to fruit | | | Write Psalm on paper | Bury paper at root of a vine |
| 127 | Helping sight | | | | Read Psalm |
| 128 | Banishing ghosts | | Blade of grass, water | Write Psalm on grass | Wash grass with water then sprinkle house |
| 129 | Blessing a house or field | | | Write Psalm with Psalm 109 on 4 cards | Bury cards at corners of house or field |
| 130 | Preventing bad dreams | | | Write Psalm on paper | Attach paper to right arm |
| 131 | Catching fish | | | Write Psalm on paper | Attach paper to fishing nets |
| 132 | Being welcomed everywhere | Seven | Rose oil | Write on paper | Read 7 times over rose oil and rub in face |
| 133 | Increasing goods | Seven & Seven | | | Read 7 times in the morning & in the evening |

| Psalm | Purpose | Times | Ingredients | Write | Use |
|---|---|---|---|---|---|
| 134 | Healing sickness | Seven | Oil | | Read 7 times over oil and rub in face |
| 134 | Healing sick eyes | | Tuff stone, wine | | Put stone in wine, read Psalm while sick person drinks wine |
| 135 | Overcoming enemy | | | | Read Psalm in front of enemy's door |
| 136 | Stopping blood flow | Seven | Menstrual blood, myrrh | Write Psalm with husband and mother's names in blood | Perfume paper with myrrh, seal in phial with wax, bury in water flowing East, recite 7 times |
| 137 | Deliverance from prison | Seven | Rose water | Write Psalm on paper | Read 7 times over rose water, rub water on face, then attach paper to arm |
| 138 | Penitence from adultery | Seven | | | Read 7 times daily |
| 139 | To be saved from poison | Seven & Seven, times Seven | | | Read 7 times per morning & evening for 7 days |
| 140 | Protection from scoundrels | Seven | | | Recite 7 times |

| Psalm | Purpose | | | | |
|---|---|---|---|---|---|
| 141 | Release from prison | Seven & Seven | | | Read 7 times a morning & evening |
| 141 | Bringing a servant back | | | Write Psalm & Characters on paper | Hang paper in air |
| 142 | Deliverance from prison | | | Write Psalm | Read Psalm |
| 143 | Victory in combat | Seven | | Write Psalm & Characters | Carry on you |
| 143 | Assisting labour | | | | Written on hip |
| 143 | Rescue from shipwreck | | | | Read |
| 144 | Restoring a husband | Seven | Oil | Write Psalm on paper | Read 7 times over oil, rub woman's body with it, then bury paper under door |
| 144 | Healing sickness | Seven | Oil | | Read 7 times over oil then rub into face |

| | | | | | |
|---|---|---|---|---|---|
| 145 | Healing sickness including bones | Seven | Oil | | Recite 7 times over oil, rub in oil while reciting again |
| 146 | Healing sickness | Seven | Oil | | Recite 7 times over oil, rub in oil |
| 147 | Blessings for a house | | Saffron, rosewater, aloe | Write Psalm with saffron & rosewater on paper | Perfume paper with aloe, & bury in the foundations |
| 148 | Banishing demons from a house | Seven | | | Read 7 times a day |
| 148 | Healing a sick woman | Seven | Oil | | Recite over oil and rub in |
| 149 | Healing a sick woman | Seven | Oil | | Recite over oil and rub in |
| 150 | To increase wheat & oil | Seven | Wheat, oil | | Recite 7 times over the wheat & oil |

# 2. Analysis of Psalm Use by Component and Frequency

## Purpose of Charm

| Purpose | Frequency |
| --- | --- |
| Child – preventing crying/minor health issues/education | 5 |
| Combat | 2 |
| Desire/love – removing/gaining | 14 |
| Farm magic – bees/fields/livestock/seeds | 5 |
| Health issues/healing | 27 |
| High friendships – princes, nobles, judges etc | 18 |
| Killing/destroying enemies | 8 |
| Lucky/improving fortune | 15 |
| Pregnancy protection/assistance | 9 |
| Protection from/dispelling enchantment | 10 |
| Protection from malice/enemies | 15 |
| Protection or blessing of house | 9 |
| Protection when travelling | 6 |
| Release from/detaining in Prison | 9 |
| Sleep – gaining/preventing/dealing with dreams | 4 |
| Ship - stopping sailing/sinking/fishing/shipwreck rescue | 5 |
| Thief/theft – detecting | 2 |
| Vanquishing enemies | 12 |
| Vine trees & vineyards – protecting/blessing | 4 |

# INGREDIENTS FOR CHARMS

| Ingredient | Frequency |
| --- | --- |
| Aloe wood | 8 |
| Aromatic Gum | 1 |
| Barley Beer | 1 |
| Blood – bat | 1 |
| Blood – bird | 1 |
| Blood – black hen | 1 |
| Blood – dove | 2 |
| Blood – white cockerel | 1 |
| Blood – goat | 1 |
| Blood – menstrual | 1 |
| Bread | 1 |
| Borax | 1 |
| Camphor | 1 |
| Cinnamon | 1 |
| Date Stones | 1 |
| Dust/Earth | 5 |
| Egg Shell (Raw) | 1 |
| Galbanum | 1 |
| Grass (blade) | 1 |
| Incense | 4 |
| Mastic | 15 |
| Myrrh | 2 |
| Musk | 4 |
| Nutmeg | 1 |
| Saffron | 3 |
| Oil (good) | 11 |
| Oil (Holy) | 1 |

| | |
|---|---|
| Olive Oil | 4 |
| Rose Oil | 6 |
| Rose Water | 5 |
| Roses | 1 |
| Saffron | 4 |
| Salt | 1 |
| Swallow (powdered) | 1 |
| Tuff Stone | 1 |
| Water (clean/pure) | 13 |
| Water (holy) | 10 |
| Water (spring) | 3 |
| Water (a woman washed in) | 4 |
| Wheat | 1 |
| Wine | 5 |

# BASIS FOR CHARMS

| Basis | Item |
|---|:---:|
| Bronze Drinking Vessel | 1 |
| Card | 2 |
| Cooking Pot (new) | 4 |
| Drinking Glass | 1 |
| Fox Skin | 1 |
| Glass Plate | 8 |
| Earthenware Pot, Jar or Bowl (new) | 3 |
| Ink-pen – Bronze/Iron | 1 |
| Ink-pen – Gold | 1 |
| Fire | 2 |
| Leaf – Laurel | 1 |
| Leaf – Lettuce | 1 |
| Leaf – Olive | 1 |
| Linen | 1 |
| Paper | 57 |
| Parchment | 2 |
| Tablet | 4 |
| Vellum | 2 |

# FREQUENCY OF REPETITION

| Repetition | Occurrences |
|---|---|
| 1 & 1 | 1 |
| 2 & 2 | 1 |
| 3 | 4 |
| 4 | 1 |
| 7 | 49 |
| 7 & 7, or other multiples | 5 |
| 20 | 1 |

# 3. The Uses of Psalm 118 in Sefer Shimmush Tehillim

The *Sepher Shimmush Tehillim* gives numerous different uses for this, the longest Psalm. It is broken down into twenty-two divisions, each of eight verses corresponding to a Hebrew letter.

Aleph (verses 1-8) pronounced in a low and even tone over a man whose limbs quiver and shake. Also for those who wish to keep a vow.

Beth (verses 9-16) in order to receive an open heart and a good memory and also a desire to learn and an extended intelligence. On a Thursday evening, after fasting the entire day, shell a hard-boiled egg carefully and write the eight verses of this division as well as *Deuteronomy 33:4* and *Joshua 1:1-8* and the holy names of the angels, Chofniel (ChPhNIAL, *'Overshadow me Mighty God'*), Shuvniel (ShVBNIAL, *'Turn me again, Mighty God'*) and Mupiel (MVPhIAL, *'Out of the mouth of Mighty God'*). A prayer is also written on the egg. Then the egg is inserted whole into the mouth and eaten whole and when it is eaten, the first four verses (9-12) should be repeated three times.

Gimel (verses 17-24) in order to heal a seriously injured eye, when prayed seven times in succession.

Daleth (verses 25-32) firstly for an injured left eye, as above and secondly, for a lawsuit or a difficult change of profession. Repeat these verses eight times in succession. But if you wish to receive information and help from many people to achieve a mission successfully, repeat ten times.

Heh (verses 33-40) written on deerskin parchment and hung around the neck will prevent a man from committing sins.

Vav (verses 41-48) will ensure an obedient nd willing servant if spoken over water and given to them to drink.

Zain (verses 49-56). There are two properties. Firstly, when written on small piece of parchment with the holy name Raphael (RPhAL, *'Healer of God'*), it will lift the melancholy and heal a person who has become splenetic. It will also relieve severe itching on the side. Bind it over the part of the body where there Spleen lies. Secondly, when repeated eighteen times, it will help you withdraw from an undertaking that has been recommended to you by evil counsellors that promises evil results, without injury to yourself.

Cheth (verses 57-64) will cure severe pains in the upper parts of the body if spoken seven times over wine and given to the sick person.

Teth (verses 65-72) to take way hip pain or cure severe kidney or liver complaints. Pronounce eight times over a patient.

Yod (verses 73-80) to find favour with God and mankind when prayed at the close of each morning's prayers.

Kaph (verses 81-88) to cure a dangerous sore or burning swelling on the right side of your nose, when prayed ten times over the sore.

Lamed (verses 89-96) pray the night before you are summoned to appear before a Judge in a lawsuit and you will be justified.

Mem (verses 97-104) for pain in the limbs and paralysis of the right arm. Pray seven times for three successive days over the arm.

Nun (verses 105-112) to accomplish a journey in safety when prayed a few days in advance, after morning and evening prayers.

Samekh (verses 113-120) for receiving a favourable outcome to a petition from a superior.

Ayin (verses 121-128) similar to the division of the letter Mem, but now to heal pain in the left arm or hand.

Peh (verses 129-136) similar to Kaph, but this time to heal a boil or swelling on the left side of the nose.

Tzaddi (verses 137-144) for officials to give just and correct decisions, when asked of their knowledge and services. Pray three times before giving your decision.

Qoph (verses 145-153) to cure a painful and dangerous injury on the left leg. Pray over rose oil and anoint injury with the oil.

Resh (verses 153-160) pray over onion water or juice to cure a painful and constantly running boil in the right ear. Drip one drop into the ear.

Shin (verses 161-168) to cure severe or burning headaches. Pray three times over pure olive oil and anoint the place where it hurts the most.

Tav (verses 169-176) as for Resh, but to cure a boil in the left ear.

Also for those who are afflicted with pain in both arms, in the sides and in the legs at the same time should repeat the whole Psalm, reciting each division of eight verses in the following order. This remedy is apparently infallible: Aleph, Tav, Beth, Shin, Gimel, Resh, Daleth, Qoph, Heh, Tzaddi, Vav, Peh, Zain, Ayin, Cheth, Samekh, Teth, Nun, Yod, Mem, Kaph, Lamed.

For searing pain in the loins, make knots in magical water at the end of the Psalm in the names of: Adam, Seth, Enoch, Canaan, Mahalleel, Jared, Methusaleh, Lamech, Noah and Shem.

# 4. PENTACLES FROM THE KEY OF SOLOMON THE KING

These Pentacles are numbered based on their position in the book *The Key of Solomon the King* by S.L. MacGregor Mathers, Redway, 1889 (available in various editions). This book was a compilation from seven different manuscripts of the *Key of Solomon* including *Lansdowne MS 1202*. Note the planetary sequence was adjusted by Mathers to follow the Qabalistic sequence down the Sephiroth of the Tree of Life from Binah (Saturn) to Yesod (Moon).

| Pentacle | Figure No. | Pentacle | Figure No. |
|---|---|---|---|
| Saturn 1 | 11 | Mars 6 | 30 |
| Saturn 2 | 12 | Mars 7 | 31 |
| Saturn 4 | 14 | Sun 4 | 35 |
| Saturn 7 | 17 | Sun 5 | 36 |
| Jupiter 2 | 19 | Sun 6 | 37 |
| Jupiter 3 | 20 | Sun 7 | 38 |
| Jupiter 4 | 21 | Venus 5 | 43 |
| Jupiter 6 | 23 | Mercury 5 | 48 |
| Jupiter 7 | 24 | Moon 1 | 49 |
| Mars 3 | 27 | Moon 2 | 50 |
| Mars 4 | 28 | Moon 3 | 51 |
| Mars 5 | 29 | Moon 5 | 53 |

# 5. PENTACLES FROM VERITABLE KEY OF SOLOMON

These Pentacles are numbered based on their position within the manuscript Wellcome MS 4670, which was reproduced as part of *The Veritable Key of Solomon*, by Stephen Skinner & David Rankine, Golden Hoard, 2008 & Llewellyn, 2009.

| Pentacle | MS Page | Pentacle | MS Page |
|---|---|---|---|
| Sun 1 | 56 | Mars 10 | 118 |
| Sun 2 | 57 | Mercury 1 | 135 |
| Sun 4 | 59 | Mercury 2 | 136 |
| Sun 5 | 60 | Mercury 4 | 139 |
| Sun 6 | 61 | Mercury 5 | 140 |
| Sun 8 | 63 | Mercury 7 | 142 |
| Sun 12 | 68 | Mercury 10 | 145 |
| Moon 1 | 83 | Jupiter 1 | 160 |
| Moon 4 | 87 | Jupiter 2 | 162 |
| Mars 1 | 108 | Jupiter 6 | 166 |
| Mars 2 | 109 | Venus 5 | 188 |
| Mars 3 | 111 | Saturn 1 | 207 |
| Mars 4 | 112 | Saturn 5 | 211 |
| Mars 5 | 113 | Saturn 8 | 214 |
| Mars 8 | 116 | | |

# 6. Planetary Hours

The planetary hours are attributed in a set sequence to the days of the week, with the hours of daylight (and night) divided into twelve equal quantities (which are usually more or less than an hour long). For more details of how to calculate planetary hours see *Practical Planetary Magick* by David Rankine & Sorita d'Este, Avalonia, 2007.

| Planetary Hours of the Day | | | | | | |
|---|---|---|---|---|---|---|
| Hour | Sun | Mon | Tues | Wed | Thurs | Fri | Sat |
| 1 | Sun | Moon | Mars | Mercury | Jupiter | Venus | Saturn |
| 2 | Venus | Saturn | Sun | Moon | Mars | Mercury | Jupiter |
| 3 | Mercury | Jupiter | Venus | Saturn | Sun | Moon | Mars |
| 4 | Moon | Mars | Mercury | Jupiter | Venus | Saturn | Sun |
| 5 | Saturn | Sun | Moon | Mars | Mercury | Jupiter | Venus |
| 6 | Jupiter | Venus | Saturn | Sun | Moon | Mars | Mercury |
| 7 | Mars | Mercury | Jupiter | Venus | Saturn | Sun | Moon |
| 8 | Sun | Moon | Mars | Mercury | Jupiter | Venus | Saturn |
| 9 | Venus | Saturn | Sun | Moon | Mars | Mercury | Jupiter |
| 10 | Mercury | Jupiter | Venus | Saturn | Sun | Moon | Mars |
| 11 | Moon | Mars | Mercury | Jupiter | Venus | Saturn | Sun |
| 12 | Saturn | Sun | Moon | Mars | Mercury | Jupiter | Venus |

| Planetary Hours of the Night | | | | | | |
|---|---|---|---|---|---|---|
| Hour | Sun | Mon | Tues | Wed | Thurs | Fri | Sat |
| 1 | Jupiter | Venus | Saturn | Sun | Moon | Mars | Mercury |
| 2 | Mars | Mercury | Jupiter | Venus | Saturn | Sun | Moon |
| 3 | Sun | Moon | Mars | Mercury | Jupiter | Venus | Saturn |
| 4 | Venus | Saturn | Sun | Moon | Mars | Mercury | Jupiter |
| 5 | Mercury | Jupiter | Venus | Saturn | Sun | Moon | Mars |
| 6 | Moon | Mars | Mercury | Jupiter | Venus | Saturn | Sun |
| 7 | Saturn | Sun | Moon | Mars | Mercury | Jupiter | Venus |
| 8 | Jupiter | Venus | Saturn | Sun | Moon | Mars | Mercury |
| 9 | Mars | Mercury | Jupiter | Venus | Saturn | Sun | Moon |
| 10 | Sun | Moon | Mars | Mercury | Jupiter | Venus | Saturn |
| 11 | Venus | Saturn | Sun | Moon | Mars | Mercury | Jupiter |
| 12 | Mercury | Jupiter | Venus | Saturn | Sun | Moon | Mars |

# BIBLIOGRAPHY

Agrippa, Cornelius. *The Fourth Book of Occult Philosophy.* London, Askin Press, 1978

Arnovick, Leslie K. *Written Reliquaries: the Resonance of Orality in Medieval English Texts.* Amsterdam, John Benjamins Publishing Co, 2006

Baker, Colin F. & Meira Polliack (eds). *Arabic and Judaeo-Arabic Manuscripts in the Cambridge Genizah Collections.* Cambridge, Cambridge University Press, 2001

Banck, A. *Byzantine Art in the Collections of the USSR.* Moscow, ND.

Betz, Hans Dieter (ed). *The Greek Magical Papyri in Translation.* Chicago, Chicago university Press, 1992

Bohak, Gideon. *Ancient Jewish Magic: A History.* Cambridge, Cambridge University Press, 2008

Boustan, Ra'anan S., & Annette Yoshiko Reed (ed). *Heavenly Realms and Earthly Realities in Late Antique Religions.* Cambridge, Cambridge University Press, 2004

Bremmer, Jan & Jan R. Veestra (eds). *The Metamorphosis of Magic from Late Antiquity to the Early Modern Period.* Paris, Peeters, 2002

Chajes, Jeffrey Howard. *Between Worlds: Dybbuks, Exorcists and Early Modern Judaism.* Pennsylvania, Pennsylvania State University Press, 2003

Collins, Derek. *Magic in the Ancient Greek World.* Oxford, Blackwell Publishing Ltd, 2008

Daiches, Samuel. *Babylonian Oil Magic in the Talmud and in the later Jewish Literature.* Jews College, London, 1913

Daniel, R.W. *A Christian Amulet on Papyrus.* Vigiliae Christianae 37.4 (1983), 400-404

Davies, Owen. *Cunning-Folk. Popular Magic in English*

*History.* London, Hambledon & London, 2003

Dennis, Rabbi Geoffrey W. *The Encyclopedia of Jewish Myth, Magic and Mysticism.* Minnesota, Llewellyn, 2007

Duling, Dennis C. *Solomon, Exorcism, ad the Son of David.* Harvard Theological Review 68.3/4 (1975), 235-252

Flint, Valerie I.J. *The Rise of Magic in Early Medieval Europe.* New Jersey, Princeton University Press, 1991

Gaster, Moses. *Studies and Texts in Folklore, Magic, Medieval Romance, Hebrew Apocrypha and Samaritan Archaeology.* New Jersey, KTAV Publishing Inc, 1990

Hazard, Willis Hatfield. *A Syriac Charm.* Journal of the America Oriental Society 15 (1893), 284-296

Hedegård, Gösta. *Liber Iuratus Honorii.* Stockholm, Almqvist & Wiksell International, 2002

Herrmann, Klaus. *Jewish Mysticism in the Geonic Period.* In *Officina Magica.* Leiden, Brill, 2005, 171-212

Jeffers, Ann. *Magic and Divination in Ancient Palestine and Syria.* Leiden, Brill, 1996

Kennedy, Patrick. *Legendary Fictions of the Celts.* London, Macmillan, 1891

Kieckhefer, Richard. *Forbidden Rites. A Necromancer's Manual of the Fifteenth Century.* Stroud, Sutton Publishing, 1997

Klein, Michele. *A Time to Be Born: Customs and Folklore of Jewish Birth.* Philadelphia, Jewish Publication Society, 1998

Klutz, Todd (ed). *Magic in the Biblical World: From the Rod of Aaron to the Ring of Solomon.* London, T&T Clark International, 2003

Kraus, Thomas J. (ed). *Ad Fontes. Original Manuscripts and Their Significance for Studying Early Christianity.* Leiden, Brill, 2007

Kruger, Michael J. *The Gospel of the Savior: An Analysis of P.Oxy.840 And Its Place in the Gospel Traditions of Early Christianity.* Leiden, Brill, 2005

MacDonald, Michael Albion (ed). *De Nigromancia*

*(attributed to) Roger Bacon*. New Jersey, Heptangle Books, 1988

MacLeod, Mindy, & Bernard Mees. *Runic Amulets and Magic Objects*. Suffolk, Boydell Press, 2006

Maguire, Henry (ed). *Byzantine Magic*. Dumbarton Oaks, Washington D.C., 1995

Marcos, Natalio Fernández & Wilfred G.E. Watson (trans). *The Septuagint in Context: Introduction to the Greek Version of the Bible*. Leiden, Brill, 2000

Mathers, S. Liddell MacGregor (trans., ed.). *The Key of Solomon the King (Clavicula Salomonis)*. London, Routledge & Kegan Paul Ltd, 1976

Mathiesen, Robert. *Magic in Slavia Orthodoxa: The Written Tradition*. In *Byzantine Magic*, Washington, 1995:155-77

McLean, Adam (ed), Fiona Tait & Christopher Upton & Dr J.W.H. Walden (trans). *The Steganographia of Trithemius*. Edinburgh, Magnum Opus, 1982.

Meyer, Marvin W., & Richard Smith. *Ancient Christian Magic: Coptic Texts of Ritual Power*. Princeton, Princeton University Press, 1999

Mirecki, Paul A., & Marvin W. Meyer. *Magic and Ritual in the Ancient World*. Leiden, Brill, 2002

Naveh, Joseph, & Shaul Shaked. *Amulets and Magic Bowls: Aramaic Incantations of Late Antiquity*. Jerusalem, Magnes Press, 1998

Peters, John P. *The Psalms as Liturgies*. Charleston, BiblioLife, 2009

Peterson, Joseph (ed). *The Sixth and Seventh Books of Moses*. Florida, Ibis Press, 2008

Peterson, Joseph (ed). *John Dee's Five Books of Mystery*. Maine, Red Wheel Weiser, 2003

Pollington, Stephen. *Leechcraft: Early English Charms Plantlore and Healing*. Norfolk, Anglo-Saxon Books, 2003

Prentice, William K. *Magical Formulae on Lintels of the Christian Period in Syria*. American Journal of Archaeology

10.2 (1906), 137-150

Savedow, Steve (ed). *Sepher Rezial Hemelach: The Book of the Angel Rezial.* Maine, Samuel Weiser Inc, 2000

Schiffman, Lawrence, & Michael Swartz. *Hebrew and Aramaic Incantation Texts from the Cairo Genizah.* Continuum International Publishing Group, 1992

Shaked, Shaul (ed). *Officina Magica. Essays on the Practice of Magic in Antiquity.* Leiden, Brill, 2005

Sibley, Ebenezer, & Frederick Hockley, & Joseph Peterson (ed.). *The Clavis or Key to the Magic of Solomon.* Florida, Ibis Press, 2009

Skemer, Don C. *Binding Words: Textual Amulets in the Middle Ages.* Pennsylvania, Pennsylvania State University Press, 2006

Skinner, Stephen, & David Rankine. *The Goetia of Dr Rudd.* Singapore, Golden Hoard Press, 2007

Skinner, Stephen, & David Rankine. *The Veritable Key of Solomon.* Singapore, Golden Hoard Press, 2008

Skinner, Stephen, & David Rankine & Harry Barron (trans). *A Collection of Magical Secrets*, London, Avalonia, 2009

Thomas, Northcote W. *Crystal Gazing.* New York, Dodge Publishing, 1905

Thompson, R. Campbell. *Semitic Magic: Its Origins and Development.* Maine, Samuel Weiser Inc, 2000

Trachtenberg, Joshua. *Jewish Magic and Superstition: A Study in Folk Religion.* Chicago, University of Chicago Press, 1939

Van Haelst, J. *Catalogue des Papyrus Littéraires Juifs et Chrétiens.* Paris, Publications de la Sorbonne, 1976

Vikan, Gary. *Art, Medicine and Magic in Early Byzantium.* Dumbarton Oaks Papers 38 (1984), 65-86.

Weeks, William T.M. *Charm against Witches and Evil Spirits.* Folklore 31.2 (1920), 146-47.

Worms, Abraham von, & Georg Dehn (ed) & Steven Guth (trans). *The Book of Abramelin.* Florida, Ibis Press, 2006.

# INDEX

199

Lightning Source UK Ltd.
Milton Keynes UK
UKHW02f0616220518

322981UK00002B/119/P

9 781905 297283